DATE DUE

DEMCO 38-296

Quick and EASY
Ways to Connect With Students and Their Parents,
Grades K-8

We can do no great things,
Only small things with great love.

—Mother Theresa

I dedicate this book to Bill and Wes who have always believed in me and have shown me great love in all the small things.

Diane Mierzwik

Quick and EASY
Ways to Connect With Students and Their Parents,
Grades K-8

Improving Student Achievement Through Parent Involvement

CORWIN PRESS
A Sage Publications Company
Thousand Oaks, California

For information:

Corwin Press
A Sage Publications Company
2455 Teller Road
Thousand Oaks, California 91320
www.corwinpress.com

Sage Publications Ltd.
1 Oliver's Yard
55 City Road
London EC1Y 1SP
United Kingdom

Sage Publications India Pvt. Ltd.
B-42, Panchsheel Enclave
Post Box 4109
New Delhi 110 017 India

Printed in the United States of America

Library of Congress Cataloging-in-Publication Data

Mierzwik, Diane.
Quick and easy ways to connect with students and their parents, grades K-8:
Improving student achievement through parent involvement / Diane Mierzwik.
    p. cm.
Includes index.
ISBN 0–7619–3179–1 (cloth)—ISBN 0–7619–3180–5 (pbk.)
    1. Education, Elementary—Parent Participation—United States.
2. Home and school—United States. I. Title.
LB1048.5.M54 2004
372.13—dc22   2004000415

04   05   06   07   10   9   8   7   6   5   4   3   2   1

Acquisitions Editor:	Rachel Livsey
Editorial Assistant:	Phyllis Cappello
Production Editor:	Melanie Birdsall
Copy Editor:	Annette Pagliaro
Typesetter:	C&M Digitals (P) Ltd.
Proofreader:	Tricia Lawrence
Indexer:	Kathy Paparchontis
Cover Designer:	Tracy E. Miller
Graphic Designer:	Lisa Miller

Contents

Preface

No significant learning occurs without a significant relationship.

—Dr. James Comer

It was a nice Southern California day 16 years ago, but I was nervous all the same. I had my first interview for a teaching position. I tried to think of ways to set myself apart from the other interviewees by discussing my core values as a teacher. I kept asking myself what made a good teacher.

I thought of all my teachers and wondered why some stood out while others faded quickly. I thought if I could capture the essence of what those memorable teachers had, then I could capture the attention of my interviewers.

Who were the memorable teachers? They were: Mr. Park, who told me I was the class poet; Mr. Braxton, who challenged me to rewrite a paper, to strive for excellence; Mr. Wilson, who laughed at my jokes; and Mrs. Lively, who seemed happy to see me every day. All of these teachers had something in common; they seemed to like me, to believe in me.

My interview went well and I got the job.

Nine years later my son began kindergarten. He is now in fifth grade. Which teachers will stand out for him, I wonder? I know which stand out for me. They are: Mrs. DeWees, who called as soon as Wes was misbehaving to reassure me that things would work out, but wanted me to know; Mrs. Vento, who gave extra time to Wes to tutor him in an area he was struggling with; Mrs. Usher, who always pointed out in every parent-teacher conference positive attributes Wesley exhibited; and Tamara, who expects the best from Wes. These are all teachers who communicate well and care.

As a teacher I have learned so much from teachers who made a difference in my life, and by teachers who are making a difference in my son's life. They have all influenced who I am as a teacher. I strive to be a teacher who cares for my students and who communicates with my students' parents.

The research is indisputable. The more involved the parent is with his or her child's education, the more successful that child will be in school. "If we can influence the thinking and behaviors of the parents positively, then we can effect the way our students perform at school" ("Improving Parental Involvement in Our Schools," Chancy, 2002).

The importance of communicating with parents and students about teacher expectations and student achievements is crucial. Finding ways as a teacher to reach out to students and their parents is imperative to the success of students.

This book includes activities that focus on positive interactions between you, the student, and the parent. The activities take very little time. Spending a few minutes at the end of your day to write a thank-you note to a parent who volunteered, or a post card to a student who shined that day will not only make a positive impact on the parent or student, but also will help you to focus on the good things that are happening in your class. Deciding to print a certificate each week to acknowledge a student or to make a positive phone call home will not only effect how the parent and student feel about your class, but also will effect how you feel about your class. Actively engaging students and parents in all the positive things happening in your class will improve everyone's perspective.

When I began to use the activities, I found I had fewer confrontations with students and parents, gained support from parents, motivated students, and improved my perception of my classes. I have been able to prove an increase in student homework completion, improved attendance, and improved overall grades. I also have been able to fine-tune the activities so they cost me very little time and have the greatest rewards. But would the activities work for another teacher?

I have shared these activities with my colleagues during staff meetings and they have had the same results: student motivation, parent support, and positive perceptions on their part despite our different teaching styles, philosophies, and attitudes.

This book does not ask you to make home visits, attend more after-school meetings, or to reinvent the wheel. It asks you to take those things you are already doing and fine-tune them for the greatest benefit. This book provides quick, easy ways for teachers to build relationships with students and their parents. These activities only require of you a few minutes at the end of the day. If you integrate them into your regular day, and make a habit of completing one task before you push away from your desk at the end of the day, you will be rewarded.

Some Guidelines

The first part of the book is about how to connect with students. The chapters suggest small changes in how you conduct class to make the most of every interaction with students, ways to honor students and their achievements in the class, and ways to notice each student for the complete person he or she is becoming. These connections are essential to your relationship with your students and are essential to your students' achievement in your class. Students who feel cared for are more motivated to do well in class.

The second part of the book is about how to connect with parents. Parents are the most important adults in the lives of your students. It is important for you to respect parents and to involve them in the education of their children. Many of the activities require sending documents home with students.

Finally, the last few chapters of the book are about connecting with parents, students, and the community. This section is for the overachievers among you. Once you have experienced the rewards of connecting in a meaningful way with students and parents, you will not be able to resist connecting with the community.

Not all the activities fit every teaching personality. Try them out, see which ones work for you, and then choose some that you can use regularly and easily. I believe students want to be successful, parents want to be involved, and communities want to be proud of their schools. With these activities all of this is possible.

Reference

Chancy, Holly W. (2002). *Improving Parental Involvement in Our Schools.* http://portfolios.valdosta.edu/hwchancy/discipline_pl.

Acknowledgments

The contributions of the following reviewers are gratefully acknowledged:

Dr. Theron J. Schutte
Principal
Boone Middle School
Boone, IA

Dr. Alana L. Mraz
Director of Curriculum
Lake Forest School District 67
Lake Forest, IL

John C. Hughes
Principal
Public School 48
Bronx, NY

Anne Roede Giddings
Curriculum Supervisor, 5–8
Newington Public Schools
Newington, CT

Lisa Suhr
Teacher
Sabetha Elementary School
Sabetha, KS

Sharon Jeffery
National Board Certified Teacher
Plymouth Public Schools
Plymouth, MA

Molly Burger
Assistant Principal
Middleton Middle School
Middleton, ID

Chris Merriam
Art Teacher
Kayenta Intermediate School
Kayenta, AZ

Mitzi Chizek
Principal
Dallas Center-Grimes High School
Grimes, IA

About the Author

 **Diane Mierzwik** currently teaches seventh- and eighth-grade English at Parkview Middle School for the Yucaipa-Calimesa Joint Unified School District in California. In her 15 years of teaching, she has had experience with first through twelfth graders. She has been Gifted And Talented Education Coordinator, Leadership Team Member, Department Head, a mentor teacher, and completed the Inland Empire Writing Project and served as a Language Arts Consultant for the California Language Arts Project.

PART I

Connecting With Students

1

Having Students Introduce Themselves

My third year of teaching, I was transferred to Del Vallejo Middle School as a Language Arts/Reading Teacher. It was my first experience with middle school students, but I was excited at the prospect of working on a team: a group of teachers who all share the same student population. After meeting the other members of my team and sharing ideas about beginning the school year, it became apparent that everyone was going to do the same thing: hand out rules, go over procedures, and distribute books. I thought about how boring the first day of school must be for a student, doing the same thing all day. I decided I would try something different. Although procedures, rules, and books are all important, I wanted to ensure that my students would still be listening to me by the third period.

I came up with an activity that required minimal class control, having not established any yet, and allowed me time to get to know my students. I assigned an acrostic poem. Students were to use each letter of their names to find an adjective that described themselves. I handed out dictionaries, did an example using my last name, explained expectations for behavior during the activity, and then let the students begin. Once a student had completed the assignment on notebook paper, he received construction paper and markers to make a poster of the poem for the back wall.

It turned out to be a wonderful day. Students were on-task. I had my classroom wall ready for Back-to-School Night. In addition, I was already able to tell the difference between Jon and John in my second period class because we had a discussion about using the same adjectives. Since both students had the same letters in their names, could they both use the same adjectives. Was that cheating? By the end of the day, I was energized when I went to the staff room for a quick debriefing meeting with my team.

One of the first topics that came up was a student named Freddy. Everyone was commenting on how he was already belligerent in class and would need our complete support if he was to be successful on our team. I was a bit concerned that I didn't even remember Freddy. I found his name in my roll book and noted that he had been in my class. (Someone suggested he might have ditched my class because I *would have remembered him.*) The meeting continued with some other business and then we all dispersed, heading back to our classrooms to get ready for the next day.

As soon as I returned to my classroom, I found Freddy's poem. It read:

Fatherless

Reckless

Energetic

Daring

Dumb

Young

I grabbed the poem and went to the counselor's office and asked her what she could tell me about Freddy. She shared with me that Freddy's father had been murdered over the summer break. The father was approached at a supermarket and shot for no apparent reason. I wandered to each of my teammates' classrooms and shared this information. Each teacher was astonished and then sympathetic. We all had a new perception of who Freddy was and what Freddy needed from us as his teachers.

The poem activity shed light on a part of Freddy's life that I, as his teacher, might never have known, or I might have found out after I had established a relationship with Freddy that was confrontational or authoritarian in an attempt to establish myself as the leader of the classroom. As it was, Freddy had willingly shared this private matter with me, allowing the rest of his teachers and I to approach him as an individual with individual needs.

Since this first experience, I have always begun my year with an activity that enables students to share with me who they are. Usually the results are not so dramatic, but I have found that it is a great opportunity to connect with students as individuals the very first time you meet them.

The following year every teacher on my team did an activity similar to mine, but adjusted it to their curriculum, available supplies, or needs. They all found it rewarding to have incorporated such an activity into their teaching.

Getting to Know Your Students

The first step in connecting with your students is getting to know them. You have a class list of names. Who better to tell you about your students than your students themselves? Plan an activity that gives students the opportunity to not only show you what they know but also who they are.

Many teachers have students introduce themselves to the class by standing up and stating their name. Some teachers have students complete a whole class activity in which they meet other students. These are great, but I like to have students complete an activity that will result in a document, the first to go on the wall for Back-to-School Night, and the first to place in their portfolios.

Having students complete an assignment allows the students to show you many things: what they know, how they are able to show what they know, and who they are. The assignment also is unthreatening. If you begin the class with "stand up and introduce yourself," you may alienate students who are shy or afraid to stand up in front of strangers. If you begin class with a "mixer" in which students are able to mix with other students you create a precedent of chaos before you have established classroom control. An individual activity allows for you to establish that classroom time will be spent on productive, student-directed activities with teacher guidance. It also sends the message to students that you are interested in who they are as individuals, how they see themselves, and the type of contribution they will make in class.

Preparing for Introduction Activities

It is important to make the directions very clear when introducing this beginning-of-the-year activity. It is also essential to confirm that you have all the necessary supplies and that the activity is appropriate for your grade level and discipline if you teach upper grades. Having all these things in place sets a tone for your class: You are indicating that you are in charge and prepared as the teacher. You are also enabling your students to successfully fulfill your expectations.

It is also very important during this time to be available for students during their work time. Once students have begun the activity, you need to be circulating through the room, commenting on progress, clarifying directions, managing supplies, and speaking with students about how you might already know them. Your students will get a clear message that you are a hands-on, approachable teacher. If students need clarification about the assignment, your availability to answer questions and give further instructions demonstrates to students that you expect each of them to be successful—with your help if necessary.

Finally, the most important element of the activity is that it is engaging while also being appropriate. Notice that my acrostic poem is an activity that many students have been exposed to before: Every child at my grade level has been introduced to the concept of adjectives and also should be familiar with how to use a dictionary. Despite all this background experience and information, I still need to support students through the activity to ensure that they are all successful.

When planning to use an activity at the beginning of the year, be sure you have chosen one that all of your students can accomplish. If you are teaching kindergarten or first grade, this may be more difficult. You may want to simply have students draw a picture of their families or something they like to do. If you teach older students, then there are many possibilities. The following is a list of activities I have seen used successfully, organized by subject matter.

English

- Acrostic poem using name

History

- Timeline of child's summer

Math

- Describe which number you are most like and why

Science

- Describe how to make you happy in the form of an experiment listing supplies and procedures

---

Obviously, there are many other activities you could use, but these examples introduce an important concept within a curricular area, rely on previous knowledge, are easily modeled, and allow students flexibility in introducing themselves through the assignment.

Allowing students the opportunity to make a first impression on you with an assignment gives them the opportunity to immediately connect with you on a personal level. In addition, you are able to get to know students in a nonthreatening manner.

Things to Remember

- Make the assignment appropriate for your students
- Provide clear instructions and an example for students
- Provide all supplies needed for this assignment
- Rely on students' previous knowledge and experiences to help them feel capable
- Circulate the room, making yourself available to students during the activity
- Post all assignments on the wall (not just the best) for Back-to-School Night

2

Greeting Students

Cashiers in high-end stores are taught to look at your credit card or check, read your name, and thank you by name. Wal-Mart was one of the first budget retailers who took a cue from high-end businesses. With as many customers as Wal-Mart has to see each day to make a profit, it would be impossible to build a personal relationship with each of its customers. Thus they did the next best thing. They made sure every customer was greeted at the door by an employee. I like this method because if I'm in a hurry, I can politely nod. If I happen to be in a friendly mood, I can say hello. There isn't a pretend relationship between you and a salesperson; there is, however, a feeling as soon as you walk in the door that you are valued as a customer.

When you feel welcome and special at a store, you are more likely to come back and shop with them again, but you have a choice. Teachers, on the other hand, have a captive audience. Despite the students' lack of choice, we still want our students to feel welcome and that they'd like to return to our classroom.

Greeting students each day by name is an important step in creating a relationship with your students. You may be the first person that day to even smile at the child and to say hello personally to the child. The effort you make each day by standing outside your door to say hello sends a clear message that you are happy to be in class and that you are happy the students are there.

Standing in the Best Place

It is important to place yourself just outside the door. This way you can see students as they approach your classroom, and simultaneously see into the classroom in case your attention is needed there. If you begin the school year standing outside the door in this manner, you send the message that you are able to monitor both areas at the same time. Students will know that you are paying attention from the beginning and be less likely to take advantage of a classroom with little supervision. The first few days, perhaps weeks, students tend to be on their best behavior and will behave appropriately in the classroom. Then it becomes a habit.

If you aren't able to begin the year in this manner, it is still important to stand outside the door. Realize, however, that there may be times when you must abandon your position outside the door to handle misbehavior inside the classroom. If this happens, make it a point to apologize to those students who were not greeted, pointing out that your attention was needed elsewhere, without giving specifics. The students who demanded your attention will get the message.

Greeting Every Child

Saying good morning or good afternoon to each and every student may end up sounding like a broken record, especially before you know your students very well. It's okay. First of all, the students will drift in at various times, giving you a break and giving them the impression that you may have greeted others in a different manner.

Making eye contact with each student is important, but be prepared for some of the students to not return the eye contact. Don't take it personally or demand that every child look at you. Just like some days at Wal-Mart when I'm in a hurry or preoccupied, my polite nod is not meant to be offensive or rude. The nod just indicates that I'm busy. Remember that some days students will be receptive to your greeting and other days students will take it for granted. As the teacher, it is up to you to be consistent.

Shaking hands with students as they enter the class may be a good idea, depending on your situation. Many conference leaders insist that it is a good way to make bodily contact with each student; it forces you and the student to slow down and acknowledge each other and gives the impression that you are in charge and mean business. I have found that, for my personality, not shaking hands works better. Greeting the students with a simple hello and smile or nod of the head does plenty for both of us, yet it doesn't require that I push my students into a possibly uncomfortable interaction.

Making the Greeting Personal

Once you've learned your students' names, it is a great idea to say hello to them personally.

At the beginning of the year, it even becomes a game in which I try to remember as many of my students' names as quickly as possible. If I'm having trouble with a name, I ask the student to remind me and then to tell me something about himself that will help me to remember his name. Not only will you have learned the student's name away from the seating chart, but you will also have made a personal connection with the student.

Once you have learned your students' names, try to make their daily greeting personal. Comment on their outfit or hairstyle. Ask about the game last night or how church group went. Asking personal questions helps your students feel that you are interested in them—not just while they are in your class, but as people who have other activities in their lives. Everyone wants to feel that someone is paying attention to them. This is a good way to make your students feel connected to you.

Managing Your Greeting Time

You are going to have a student or students who insist on talking to you as you are trying to greet other students. It is important that you explain to the student that you don't have time to talk to her now because you are saying hello to everyone and that you will discuss the situation with her later.

As mentioned earlier, you may have students who decide to try their luck inside the classroom because they think you are distracted with business outside the classroom. It is important to immediately stop greeting students and stop whatever misbehavior is occurring inside the classroom. Students should get the message that you are still insistent that they behave appropriately inside the classroom, even when they don't have your full attention.

Standing outside your door puts you in the position of seeing activities occurring in the halls. Sometimes those activities will require your attention. Once again, it is important that you abandon greeting students to address any behavioral issues in the hall. By doing so, you send your students the message that you are a leader not only in the classroom but also on campus. You are also letting other students know that they need to behave in the hall.

Creating a Healthy Climate at Your School

Administrators love teachers who help monitor the halls. It cuts down on the amount of behavior problems when there is an attentive adult present. It also helps improve the atmosphere of the school campus to have school leaders monitoring all students.

Former students will also have a chance to say hello. It is always a pleasure for a teacher to see a past student. It is great for a student to see a teacher with whom they had a good relationship, especially when that student is having a bad day. You have been a positive influence on your students and standing outside your door helps you to continue that relationship with these students.

Once you have made a habit of greeting students, you will be able to take a day off from doing so in order to handle a phone call or to help a student with make-up work. But be prepared for students to ask you where you were and for you to miss making that first connection with your students.

Beginning each day by greeting your students sets the tone for your class. It indicates to your students that they are welcome in your class, that you are happy to see them, and that you feel connected to them as people. Just a few minutes each day helps class time run smoothly.

Things to Remember

- Learn your students' names
- Say hello to every student even if the student does not respond
- Don't allow a student to monopolize this time
- Be sure to continue to expect and monitor appropriate behavior

3

Making the Most of Classroom Time

My fourth year of teaching, I attended a night performance of our school's choir. I sat in the auditorium and searched for the faces of my students. I even recognized a few students from last year's classes and made a mental note to also say hello to those students after the performance.

When the performance was over, I loitered near my seat. As my students walked by, I said hello and told them how proud I was of each of them. A young lady approached me and said hello. I smiled warmly and returned the greeting, but it must have been obvious from the look on my face that I had no idea who this girl was. She asked me, "You don't know who I am, do you?"

I looked her in the face and tried to place where I knew her from. Now, I am a person who is very good with names, unlike my husband who seems at times to forget my name after 18 years of marriage. And if I forget a name, I often still recognize the face and can place it. But, this time, I was drawing a blank.

"Ms. Mierzwik, I was in your class last year."

Tiffany went on to remind me that she had been in my class fourth period and I began to make excuses, asking things like, "Did you transfer in midyear?" "Did you transfer out?" Finally, I tried to blame her for my poor memory, "You must have been a quiet, good kid." She agreed that she was and I felt awful.

So often the quiet, good kids get lost in the shuffle. You don't have to nag them about their homework. You don't meet with their parents about their grades or poor behavior. You don't remind them to turn around and be quiet. They sit in class every day, are attentive, complete their work, and are basically ignored. Tiffany was one of those kids and I felt awful that I had done such a bad job as her teacher.

Now, there are many reasons you might forget a student from one year to the next. But there is no excuse for not making time in your day to connect with every student in your classroom over the course of the year. With all the demands placed on your time, this can be a challenge and requires that you make the most of each minute of classroom time.

Your top priority each day in class needs to be to have at least one individual interaction with each student. If you are greeting students at the door, this is a good place to begin. It would be preferable, however, if you could also create opportunities for more meaningful interactions.

All the research indicates that effective teachers make the most of instructional time. To avoid compromising your instructional time, you want to make your individual interactions tie into your instructional time. There are several ways to do this.

Handing Back Papers

We all know sponge activities, activities related to the curriculum that students can complete on their own, are the best way to start a class. It gives us time to take roll and to handle any administrative duties while students are on-task doing something valuable. A good use of this time is to hand back papers to students. It may be easier to have a student or parent volunteer do this task, but it is worth your effort to do it yourself for many reasons.

Handing back papers yourself on a regular basis helps you to connect how a student is doing in your class with the actual student. If when you hand back a paper, you look at the grade a student earned and then the student, you will associate a certain level of accomplishment with each child. If a child rises above his normal level of accomplishment, you have the opportunity when handing back the papers to congratulate him personally on it. If he drops below, you immediately have the chance to find out if there is something he needs help with. Students are given mini-conferences weekly regarding their performance in your class using this technique.

Another helpful occurrence when you are handing papers back yourself is the opportunity to personally clarify grades for students. Usually you can interpret body language when a student is unhappy about a grade. Students also will raise their hands for clarification. I've even had students complain loudly when I was still standing at their table, as if I couldn't hear them. These are great opportunities to give students immediate feedback about how well they met the expectations of the assignment and what they could do differently next time to earn a higher grade.

Finally, this time allows you to check in with students who either have been absent or just seem out of sorts. There have been many times when I have asked a student if she was okay, only to have her burst into tears. It was obvious to me that something was wrong from her body language. Apparently, however, I was the first person to ask and she was grateful for my concern.

Handing back papers to students gives you time to also be monitoring and helping students with the sponge activity. There are so many possibilities for one-on-one interaction regarding a student's progress in class, it is well worth the effort.

With younger grades, kindergarten through third grade, you may want to use this time to teach organizational skills. Having students retrieve their folder and place all returned work in the folder teaches students to keep returned work organized rather than crumpling these papers into their backpack. Parents will appreciate the organized folder. Students will learn that returned work is not throw-away work. You will provide your students time to learn valuable skills in remaining organized and yourself time to monitor students, their work, and their folders.

Collecting Work

Efficiency is the name of the game. You've probably trained your students to hand papers up their row, or to the top of their tables. This is an excellent idea when collecting daily assignments or homework. However, when you are collecting a major project it is important to collect the projects individually. As with handing back papers, you can prepare for this time by having students engage in an activity they routinely complete. Once they are working diligently, either walk around the room collecting the assignment, or have students approach you at your desk to hand-in the assignment. If the assignment is large and difficult to collect, I have students approach me. Otherwise, I collect assignments by walking around to students so I can also be monitoring their progress on the task at hand.

By collecting these larger assignments individually, you have the opportunity to congratulate each student who turns the assignment in and to admonish or check-in with those students who do not. Students quickly get the message that if they choose not to turn in an assignment, they are going to have to face you immediately and may also receive an immediate consequence for not being responsible about the assignment. I also keep a list of students who fail to turn-in an assignment as a reminder to myself to ask for the assignment the next day. I ask the student what I can do to help them complete the assignment, either assign an afterschool tutorial time with the intent of helping the student complete the assignment at that time, or make a phone call home that night to request parental support. It should not be acceptable to skip an assignment; the teacher should do everything to support students in their efforts to get assignments done.

Collecting large assignments individually gives you the opportunity to engage students immediately, privately, and individually about their progress in class. You have the chance to offer support to those students who failed to complete the assignment and to offer congratulations to those students who were responsible with the assignment.

Commenting on Student Work

Another excellent way to connect with students about their progress in class is with the use of what I call "sandwich comments." It is very easy to write a grade at the top of an assignment, especially if you have created a clear grading rubric that allows students to see exactly where and why they have earned points. This type of feedback is important for students to understand how well they are meeting the expectations of the class. A sandwich comment is a personal note from you about the assignment that says what you liked about the assignment, where you thought improvement was needed, and one other thing you liked about the assignment.

When I decided to become a teacher, I thought back to all my teachers and wondered which ones had the greatest effect on me. There were two, both of whom sang my praises. Not that I did everything right in their classes, but the clear message I received from these teachers was that I was capable and that they expected me to meet their expectations.

A sandwich comment allows you to do this for each of your students. Using their specific work allows you to indicate to them that they are capable, and it shows your students how they can continue to meet your high expectations of them. A sandwich comment could look like this:

> I loved the humor in this essay. The story you tell about your grandpa as the lead-in to the topic of aging was a great hook. It captured my interest right away and made me smile.
>
> I wanted to find out more about your grandpa throughout the essay because this is what made the topic come alive for me. Perhaps use an example from his experiences with each major point.
>
> Your conclusion was strong. Your emphasis on how we choose to either react to ageism or ignore it was a good one. I enjoyed reading this.

The personal note from you points out to the student what he or she did right, twice. This is so important because too often in school students are only told what they need to improve. In order for us to feel capable, we must know what we are doing correctly. This allows us to revisit these strengths for future assignments, build on these strengths, and use the confidence we gain from these strengths to improve our weaknesses. Students learn much more from your personal comments on their assignments than they do from the letter grade or point value.

It is important to remember when making personal comments that you must be specific when you point out what the student did right. Notice that I generally acknowledge the technique the student used correctly, then point specifically to the part of the assignment that indicates he did this correctly. Without this specific reference, students gain a vague sense that they did something right, but may not be able to repeat the success because they are unclear of where they used the technique correctly. Also, the general reference and then the specific reference help the student connect accepted terminology to their specific work.

Personal comments on student work are not easy the first few times you try to use them. It takes time to think about each child's work and what specifically you liked about it. But, with practice, this does become a natural part of your grading and you automatically can pick out strengths and articulate those for students using just a few seconds per assignment. The pay-off is huge for the student.

Writing to the Teacher

Another very effective way to connect personally with students is to have them write to you. Some teachers use journals; however, I find journals difficult to manage. Just the stack of journals, their bulk, is overwhelming to me. I prefer to do timed writings. Students write for several minutes. I provide them with the choice of either my assigned topic or a topic of their choice. They write on a single piece of paper so all I have to manage is a stack of papers that I can carry anywhere with me to read and do a written response.

Timed writings allow students a chance to write to me personally. I don't grade the papers for grammar, punctuation, or usage. The points are all or nothing. But I find out so much about my students and it allows them to write with no pressure, a chance to express themselves with me.

I use the book *Writing Down the Bones* for my topics. This book is written for adult writers, so you may need to either make some adjustments or be careful about which chapters to use. Many of my colleagues use this exercise but provide "journal topics" which work just as well. The point of the exercise is for children to have nonthreatening experiences with writing and for you to get to know your students better.

Many times students will tell me about their hobbies, families, or past experiences—which gives me a fuller picture of who they are as people. I try to do the activity once a week. If I miss, my students always remind me because they enjoy the activity so much. I limit my comments to one or two sentences, usually a question asking the student to expand on the information they have provided or I share a similar experience, like "I have a younger sister, too, who use to drive me crazy." Asking for students to expand on information indicates to them that you are interested in them and their lives. Sharing similar experiences with your students helps them to see you as someone they could relate to.

Some teachers are reluctant to try this assignment for a couple of reasons. First, they are afraid of receiving more information about a child than they want to know. My answer is that we are there to help students and if you find out something alarming about a child through timed writings, you have support staff to help you get that child help. Second, teachers are overwhelmed by the prospect of reading the papers each week. Trust me, it is fast reading because you aren't checking the assignments for spelling, grammar, or punctuation. In addition, the reading is enjoyable, kind of like getting a short note from your friend.

Many studies have shown that one of the best things for kids to do when they are trying to make sense of the world is to keep a journal

(Klein, 1999; Fellows, 1994). Writing things down has a way of putting things into perspective. Having a caring adult as their audience further helps children to feel validated. I challenge you to try this activity. You will gain a new perspective on many of your students and they will learn much from the activity.

Initiating Informal Student-Teacher Conferences

Another way to talk to your students individually is to schedule conferences with them. The conferences can be scheduled during class time, when other students are completing work, but this can be difficult to manage for many teachers. I suggest scheduling meetings before and after school, during school breaks including lunchtime, or during your scheduled time for conferences.

The conference only needs to last four or five minutes. The purpose of the conference is simply for you to ask the student how he or she thinks things are going. If you are keeping a portfolio for each student, you could use this time to review the portfolio. I prefer to keep the conference more personal.

I like to ask students how they feel about the class, pointing out for the student what I see as his or her strengths in the class. I ask the student if there is something I can do differently that would make class more engaging. Then I end on a personal note, asking about the upcoming weekend or latest dance recital, for example.

A third-grade teacher in my district plans "Lunch With the Teacher" dates as her informal conferences. She schedules one day a week when she invites a student to eat lunch with her in the classroom. This allows her time to talk to the student individually. Once they are done eating and talking, the student goes outside for the remainder of the lunch recess, so the teacher still has time to take a personal break.

This conference time is really a time for you to connect with the student without distractions. It sends a message to the students that they are worth your time and a valuable part of your class. The conference lets students know that you care about how they are doing in your class. If you plan just one conference a week with one student, it will be well worth your effort.

Using Non-Instructional Time

Good teachers also connect with their students outside of instructional time. When I see a student in the hall, even if I'm engaged in a conversation with a colleague, I smile and wave. Before and after class and during breaks, I make myself available to students for short conversations. Waving to children in the cafeteria, or as they make their way onto the school bus are important ways to create relationships with your students in which they feel comfortable with you. You become approachable when you are friendly with students outside of the classroom.

Students want to be successful in all they do. By making small changes in how you use your time at school, you will establish positive rapport with them—making them more confident in their abilities and more successful in your class.

Things to Remember

- Good teachers make the most of instructional time
- Always make yourself available to students when they are engaged in completing an assignment
- Hand back student papers yourself, paying attention to student achievement
- Be aware of student dissatisfaction with marks on their papers and be available to clarify marks
- Make personal notes on assignments to indicate what the child has accomplished
- Allow students the opportunity to communicate with you through timed writings
- Schedule personal conferences with students to check-in with them and to discuss their progress in class

---

References

Fellows, N. J. (1994). A window into thinking: Using student writing to understand conceptual changes in science learning. *Journal of Science Teaching, 31,* 985–1001.

Klein, P. D. (1999). Reopening inquiry into cognitive processes in writing-to-learn. *Educational Psychology Review, 11*(3), 203–270.

4

Congratulating Students With Certificates

The first year I decided to give out congratulations certificates, I waited until the end of the year and, true to my philosophy of finding something good in every student, I decided to give one to each student. Thus, I had to be very creative with these certificates. One certificate, for example, said the following, "Congratulations, you were the *best* at keeping the teacher on task." I gave this certificate to Amber. Whenever I got off-task in class, she would roll her eyes and exclaim, "Can we just get on with it?" Another certificate said, "Congratulations, you were the *best* at keeping your classmates on task." I gave this certificate to Bethany, the biggest tattletale in class. I was up most of the night trying to rephrase descriptions of my students into positive things so I could congratulate them for something, anything. In order to use congratulations certificates successfully, I had to rethink my planning.

Creating Certificates

There are several types of certificates you can use. Most you can find on any computer or in the back of books. Using the computer to generate certificates means you can customize the certificate to meet your needs. You may want to ask your school to invest in some quality paper to use for printing the certificates. Hopefully, you can order this through your department. If not, go to your principal, explain what you are doing, and see if there are any funds to purchase the supplies from another fund such as a parent organization or support organization.

You can create a certificate such as the following using a word processing file:

Congratulations!

_____

has received this certificate of merit for a job well done in

_____

presented on this ____ day of ____ in the year ____

by

_____

Using your word processing program, go to _page setup_ and choose _landscape_ for orientation. Then begin playing with fonts and alignment. Creating your own certificate and then saving the template on your computer make creating the certificates very easy.

There are several reasons to give out certificates. Many teachers use certificates as a means to acknowledge students who complete outstanding work. A colleague of mine assigned a math project which culminated in a poster. Once all the posters were turned in and posted, she allowed the students to vote on which poster they thought was the best. Then she did a formal presentation, handing out certificates of merit for the posters earning the most votes.

Using certificates at the end of a culminating project or unit allows you to bring closure to the unit by acknowledging outstanding work. Choosing categories for recognition is a good idea. Categories might include:

- Best overall work
- Best art work
- Best research
- Most creative
- Students' choice

Students, of course, receive a grade for their work along with your feedback on the quality of work they did throughout the project; these things are important. The point of having a presentation of certificates of merit for outstanding work is to acknowledge students who made a significant effort during the unit of work. As stated previously, it is a great way to give closure to one unit and to inspire your students for the next unit.

Another colleague of mine uses certificates at the end of each quarter to acknowledge all students who earned an A and any students who were able to bring their grade up a full letter grade from one grading period to the next. For instance, she hands out certificates to all students who earn 90% or above. She also gives certificates to students who, for example, earned a B the previous quarter and are now earning an A—or previously a C and are now a B—and so on. She understands that many A students remain A students and receive recognition in a number of ways; she also wants to encourage all students to improve and work toward earning an A in her class. The recognition of A students acknowledges her high expectations for all students. The recognition of students who have improved their grade acknowledges her belief that everyone can do better in her class.

Using certificates this way allows you to wait until all the evidence is in—grades—and then recognize those students who have done outstanding work in your class. Using the certificates at the end of each grading period requires very little time over the course of your year and once again brings closure to one grading period while inspiring for the next.

My friend who teaches art uses certificates to acknowledge all students who submit their work to any type of competition. Some competitions in her class are mandatory; others are elective. But this art teacher grew frustrated that so many students would submit work to a competition or show and only a few would receive any recognition. She began holding her own recognition ceremonies the day after the deadline for a competition or show.

She gives a speech about how the judging of art is very subjective, gives a few examples of now famous artists who were ignored during their lifetime, and then expresses how proud she is of every student who took the risk to submit work for people outside the classroom to view. She has found that within the course of the first few competitions, more students are willing to submit work to competitions and shows. In addition, those students who were already submitting work become more confident and submit pieces of art that are riskier (in that their work does not emulate a well-known artist).

I use certificates at the beginning of each week to acknowledge a person who has done something of merit. Once again, my philosophy of finding something good in every student has translated into my keeping a list of my students, keeping track of which students I have acknowledged, and going out of my way to be sure to acknowledge every student before I acknowledge a student for a second time. The first few weeks, this is relatively easy;

I believe it's because students are still trying to impress me or make a new start. Then it can become more difficult as the year progresses.

In order to acknowledge every student, you sometimes have to specifically choose a name and watch and wait for that student to accomplish something of merit. Sometimes it takes longer than one week. But if you wait, confident something good will happen, you won't be let down.

These certificates are very specific to each student. Of course, you can fall back on the tried and true such as 100% homework completion, especially if it's for a student who doesn't typically turn in all her homework. But also giving certificates to students who go out of their way to help another student, or who cooperate with you for the full week acknowledges students who otherwise may not be recognized.

Presenting Certificates

I hand out certificates on Mondays. After the completion of our sponge activity, I describe the behavior that resulted in my acknowledgment of merit, describe how this behavior will lead to future success if continued, and then call up the student who earned the certificate. I give out one certificate each week so that I am sure every student receives recognition.

Keep in mind that certificates are to be used to make a student feel proud of something he or she has done in your class. It is important that you and the other students respect the presentation of the certificates by being respectful during the presentation. Teaching students what is appropriate behavior when someone else is being recognized in class is important. Students need to be attentive and clap after the presentation, even if it is just the "polite" clap. If a teacher allows this time to be handled with a lack of respect, the certificate will have very little meaning for the student.

No matter how you decide to use certificates—you may want to experiment to see which method best meets your classroom structure—it is most important that the certificates be sincerely given for something truly worth recognition, not "best at keeping the teacher on task."

Things to Remember

- Choose to hand out certificates at regular intervals for specific purposes
- Only hand out certificates for specific, sincere recognition
- Hand out certificates during a classroom presentation
- Be sure the class knows proper etiquette for the presentation
- Provide students with envelopes in which to carry the certificates home in

5

Connecting With Your Students Through the Curriculum

Bennett was a quiet, sweet student. He was attentive in class, never disruptive or disrespectful. After three weeks of class, he had yet to turn in one piece of work. I went to his CUM file and discovered from the teacher comments that Bennett seemed to be a child who had given up. The comments began with the typical, "Bennett tries hard and is interested," progressed to "Bennett's handwriting is illegible but he continues to make an effort," until his sixth-grade teacher wrote something to the effect of "Bennett is not engaged in school."

I approached his counselor and we immediately set up an appointment to meet with his mother. She was a sweet woman with six children. Bennett was a middle child and his mother concurred that he had a very sweet disposition, but often got lost in the shuffle. She also said that there were older sisters who could help Bennett with his work. Thus I agreed to make copies of any notes Bennett was suppose to copy in class to compensate for his poor fine motor skills.

Bennett began turning in partially completed work. I praised him and gave him as many points as I could squeeze out of the work he turned in. I could see him becoming more engaged in class and more confident. It was obvious that he felt less threatened by the class. Then I collected the class's first project.

When I approached Bennett to collect his project, his desk was empty and his eyes mournful. As I began to express my disappointment, he pulled the project out from his lap. We both laughed.

I spent that weekend grading the projects. When I got to Bennett's, as usual, I squeezed as many points as I could out of what he had turned in. His grade still came out to below passing. I contemplated inflating his grade, but couldn't bring myself to do it knowing that an unearned grade is worse that no grade at all. I worried about how he was going to react to his grade.

On Monday, as I handed back the projects, I avoided Bennett's reaction for the first several minutes, keeping myself busy with handing out everyone else's projects. Finally, after I figured he had had time to process the grade, I wandered over to him.

"Bennett, are you okay?" I asked.

He nodded, not looking at me. His project was once again in his lap.

"You worked really hard on that project, didn't you?"

Again, a nod with no eye contact.

"You know, I know how you feel." Bennett finally looked at me. I pointed to above the blackboard where I had posted in large bulletin board letters "How hard are YOU trying?" below which were all my rejection slips from a summer of sending out my novel to publishers. "I send out my book over and over, knowing it's the best I can do, and still I fail. But I don't give up."

Bennett nodded his head and smiled as I got called away to another student who wanted to argue with me over five points she felt I'd cheated her. I wish I could say that Bennett gained enough confidence in my class to go on to become an A student, but he didn't. He did get tested and placed in special education so he could get the help he needed. He continued to be engaged in my class throughout the year, always doing his best. Most of all, he and I spent the year understanding one another. I knew he struggled and he knew I struggled. Whenever I'd post a new rejection slip, he'd tell *me* not to give up.

Sharing Your Personal Life With Students

Children look to adults for guidance, as role models. Teachers can be the most significant adults in children's lives outside of their family members. To be able to share a part of who you are so that students see you as a rounded human being is important to the relationship you build with students.

Oprah Winfrey loves to tell the story of how she saw one of her teachers at the supermarket and was astonished. As a child, she had no idea that teachers had lives beyond their classrooms. I like to think much has changed since then. As teachers we understand the importance of children having a full understanding of what it means to be human and to be an adult. Sharing part of our lives, beyond our teacher role, can be a great gift to our students. But, it can be a tricky thing to pull off.

Too many teachers share too much of their lives with their students, leading to parents' complaints that as teachers we are trying to unduly influence their children. We may not have the same value system as a child's family. Some of us are much more liberal than our students' families and others are much more conservative; therefore, it is important to be sure that the things we share are neutral events in our lives.

Responding to Personal Questions

Students will often ask me about my religion or how I voted in the last election. These things seem harmless enough, but I always ask why the student is asking before I give an answer to such sensitive topics. Often the question is harmless. However, there have been times when answering the question could have caused strife in my student's life and, consequently, in the life of everyone who cared about the student. It is important to be sure that the information you share about yourself will allow students to see you as a full person, not biased in one way or another.

When you engage students using your personal life, it is important to keep several things in mind. Be sure that you continue to behave in a manner that is respectful of the classroom environment and of your role as the teacher. Do not become chummy with your students. Maintain a professional distance. Be sure to allow time after you have shared for children to share their stories, either formally with the whole class, or informally with their neighbors. If you get to spend class time talking about your life, then your students should receive the same latitude. Finally, use humor when sharing your stories. Humor is the great equalizer. Being able to laugh at yourself and your mistakes gives students permission to also make mistakes and to have the opportunity to laugh about them.

A colleague of mine, who is a very private person and rather shy about talking about herself, has a bulletin board above her desk that is all about her. It has her baby picture, school pictures, wedding picture, a picture of her college graduation, and pictures of her children. All of the pictures are of milestones in her life. None of them are very personal, but all of them represent parts of her life. The pictures allow students to see her as a person beyond school without her having to talk too much about her life, which makes her uncomfortable.

Connecting Curriculum to Your Life

A friend of mine teaches math and likes to begin each unit with an illustration of how she and her family have applied the information the students are going to learn in real life. For example, a unit of measuring angles is begun with an overhead of the deck at her home. Then she passes around pictures of her and her husband building the deck and explains how important it is to be accurate with measuring the angles of the deck. While the activity relates to the curriculum, it is also a great way for students to get to know her and see pictures of her husband and her home.

Another friend of mine has shared that because she lives in the community in which she teaches, she is very careful to not share many stories. Her husband, being a very private person, actually told her that their life is off-limits. She shares stories of things she did as a child to engage her students, connecting them to books they are reading or projects they are working on through her childhood, which inevitably connects students to their own experiences.

Connecting your teaching to your life is a wonderful opportunity to teach children that things they are learning in school have applications beyond the classroom. All the best teachers begin lessons with anecdotes or jokes. These are called "hooks" in the writing world. The theory of connectionist models establishes that when students can make connections between what they are learning and something they already know, their recall and synthesis of the information, and their ability to reuse the information increases (Bereiter, 1991). By sharing your stories, students are able to connect the lesson to someone they know—you—and then make connections to other things they know. The funny thing is, when you tell a story about yourself, students often think they are getting you off-task and believe they are getting away with not doing the lesson, when actually they are becoming more engaged in the lesson. I love hearing a student in my class ask a question about how what we're learning applies to my life. They all snicker when I start to tell a story, thinking they have gotten me off-task. However, I know that they will remember my story much like I remember all of my ninth-grade Spanish teacher's, Mr. Magana, stories about helping in his father's store in Mexico and all the American customers who would come in and try to speak Spanish. He used the mistakes those customers made as reminders of how to pronounce words correctly.

The mistake teachers make in sharing their lives is sharing too much information. You must maintain your professionalism. Sharing stories that compromise your professionalism is prohibited. On the other hand, a teacher who shares nothing personal with her students because of a fear of compromising her professionalism also compromises her relationship with her students.

Whether we like it or not, we are role models for our students. Having students understand that we are well-rounded people helps them to develop into well-rounded people. It also gives them permission to give you permission to make mistakes, to have flaws, and to have likes and dislikes. Building relationships requires that each party gives a part of themselves. The relationships you build with your students will help you to motivate them and keep them engaged in the curriculum.

Things to Remember

- Connecting your life to the classroom situation must be appropriate
- Using illustrations of how curriculum fits into your life engages students
- A bulletin board of the milestones of your life is a great way to connect with students

---

Reference

Bereiter, C. (1991). Implications of connectionism for thinking about rules. *Educational Researcher, 20*(3), 10–16.

6

Recognizing Your
Students as Stars

Cheryl was a shy girl in my third-period, eighth-grade class. She did well in class, and never required any extra attention. I knew very little about her because of her introverted personality, her good work habits, and the demands of the other students. Then I attended the school's talent show.

Cheryl was in the program to sing a solo. I immediately had visions of her squeaking out a song. Although I was proud of her for having the courage to sign up for the talent show, I was also apprehensive about how this situation was going to clash with her shy personality.

It was Cheryl's turn and she stepped on stage, holding the microphone in hand. The music began and Cheryl squeaked out the first verse. During the pause before the chorus of the song began, I saw her take a deep breath and close her eyes. The next time she sang, it was with a different voice. She was confident and strong, and hit every note perfectly. The rest of the song was just as successful. I was overwhelmed by how proud I was of her. I saw her in a whole new light.

The next day in class, I mentioned to Cheryl what a great voice she had and what a great job she had done at the talent show. "You were there?" she asked, beaming. Cheryl's behavior in class changed after that. She became much more outgoing—a role model and leader for the other students. I like to think that because we connected on a personal level she was more motivated in class.

Finding Out About Your Students

I don't live in the town in which I teach, but I have a subscription to the local newspaper. It comes out once a week and is mailed directly to my house. When I receive it, I read through any article that deals with local activities that my students might be involved with. I especially look at pictures and their captions, searching for my students' names. I have found out that I have a student who is an aspiring female surfer, one who has skied across the ocean from the California coast to Catalina Island, one who is a volunteer for the local Ranger, and the list goes on. It is always exciting to find out about my students outside the realm of our time together in the classroom. It makes me see them in a new way, and it allows me to connect with them on a more personal level.

You should also read the school newspaper and school bulletin carefully for news of one of your students excelling in another area. Often you will find that one of your students is a top saxophone player, or the star basketball player, or won the state competition for Knowledge Bowl, a statewide competition testing student knowledge of curricular facts. Finding out about your students beyond your classroom helps you to see the student as a well-rounded person.

Another way to find out which activities your students are involved in is to stop by afterschool practices for activities. It only takes a few minutes to watch the practice and scan the faces for your students.

After school, stop by the football practice on your way out to your car. Stay for just a few minutes, and see if you can pick out your students. Then the next day, mention to them you saw them at practice. Or stop by the choir practice or Knowledge Bowl practice. Just being there for a few minutes and being able to strike up a conversation with the student the next day about the activity will give you a personal connection to the child. This connection will help you to motivate the student and will help the child feel valued in your classroom.

If you have more time or inclination, try to make it to outside activities. Going to school events such as a soccer game or a choir and band performance gives you a connection with those students involved. Attending other activities outside of school can also be very rewarding for you and your students.

A colleague who teaches elementary physical education attends and participates in all the local 5K runs. She announces to her students where she will be for warm-ups so that if any of them are participating she can warm up with them. She is involved in these activities anyway; spending the warm-up time with students gives her a way to connect with students.

If you are a busy person attending student activities may be difficult. If you are like me, attending your own activities is difficult enough, without having to attend someone else's activities. If you are unable to attend school games or performances, you will still want to ask how the student did if you know the student is involved.

A fourth-grade teacher in my district always asks the boy scouts in his class how the Christmas parade went even though he doesn't attend because he lives out of town. The boys are happy to share with him how much fun they had. The boys feel that the teacher is interested in them and the teacher gets to know the boys a little better.

If you are able to attend outside activities, let the student set the tone for the interaction. You may want to go out of your way to say hello and then let the student take over from there. Some students will gush with pride and introduce you to everyone they know; others will wave politely then look away. In either case, you know the child will be a different person in your class from then on because you have seen him or her as a different person.

Finally, if you are pressed for time and can't possibly attend a child's activities, strike up conversations with teachers in the staff lounge about your students. Often other teachers are a wealth of information about your students. Those teachers may know the child from being friends with the family, attending the same church or extracurricular activities, or having had them in class in previous years. Guide the conversation to how the child is unique and find out about the child's interests. Then in class mention to the student that teacher so-and-so told you about their interest or talent. Watch the child's face light up. Be sure to mention how the other teacher had all these nice things to say about the child. The child will know that you now see him or her as someone other than just another student.

Using Your Knowledge About Students

When you find an article in the paper, clip it out and make a copy of it. Create a bulletin board in class with the heading "You are a Star." Post the copy of the clipping on the bulletin board with the student's name highlighted. Give the student the actual clipping while handing back papers with a small note attached which congratulates the student and says how proud you are of the student. Some students are shy and will simply accept the clipping. Others will want to share with you about the event, activity, or organization.

What I like about the bulletin board is that students will then approach me with something they have done so I can add them to the bulletin board. The board becomes so full because almost every student has something to share. I post clippings without regard to timeliness. I don't make a production of the postings or the board. The board is there in the classroom as a constant reminder that each of us has activities outside of the classroom that we are involved in and successful with.

The other use of this information is to help students guide their choices in class. Many times as teachers we leave an assignment vague hoping that students will pursue the assignment detailing one of their interests. Then we are faced with students who say, "I don't know what to do." If you know students' interests, you can help guide their choices. I've had students who were mediocre workers, doing just enough to earn a passing grade. Then when I told them, for example, that they could apply the guidelines of the assignment to their interest in their uncle's ranch they visit every summer, their shared passion with their father for bodybuilding, or interest in fashion, these very same students have done excellent work—work I have used as exemplar in my class.

You will be able to guide your students to these choices if you see them as individuals. By not seeing a student as merely an "A student," a "B student," and so on, you can, instead, see that student as the kid taking voice lessons after school each day, the child who plays regional club soccer, or the child who plays chess competitively. Knowing this information about students helps a teacher to see beyond their poor grades on the weekly quiz, for example. Instead, teachers can view students as capable children who can do better next time. The students' knowledge that you consider them to be capable also helps them to believe that they can succeed in your class, even if they hit a road bump or two along the way.

The child has an opportunity to be someone other than your student. You have the chance to acknowledge the student for accomplishments outside of your classroom. The appreciation the student feels for the time you took to attend one of their activities helps to motivate the student in your class.

Connecting with students through their outside interests, activities, or talents allows you the opportunity to see the child as a well-rounded person. The student's knowledge that you care enough to find out about him or her will create a sense of trust between you and allow you to further motivate the child in your class. If you hit a rough spot with the child, you will have a relationship to fall back on that is larger than the classroom and may help to resolve any problems you may be having in the classroom.

I remember I had become a bully in the fourth grade. I was tormenting kids in six-square, a recess game, because no one could beat me. I wouldn't let anyone I didn't like play with my core group of friends. I also made fun of kids who tried to play with us. My fourth-grade teacher yelled at me for my behavior. When my behavior didn't change, he simply began giving me punishments that furthered my belief that I was a bully. Then my third-grade teacher came out on the playground and witnessed my behavior. She pulled me aside and said quietly, "This is not the Diane I know. What is bothering you?"

Nothing was bothering me. I was on a power high. I was beginning to see myself as a bully; my fourth-grade teacher saw me as a bully. The other kids saw me as a bully. But my third-grade teacher knew me in a different way—a better way—and assumed that something must be wrong for me to act so out of character. I immediately felt bad for letting Ms. Cameron down, and my bullying stopped.

Seeing students as well-rounded people allows us to recognize the best in them.

Things to Remember

- School newspapers, bulletins, and local papers will help you find the stars in your students
- Attending students' activities outside of the classroom gives you insight into the lives of your students
- Asking other teachers about your students will reveal information about your students
- Building relationships with students that extend beyond the classroom is invaluable

PART II

Connecting With Parents

7

Sending Home Your Introduction Letter

Before I meet students each year, I dread writing my introduction letter. How can I capture in a letter all of the nuances, accommodations, modifications, and decisions that make up the day-to-day life of a classroom with over 20 unique personalities? As the leader in the class, I must provide my students with a map of where we are going and what the rules are going to be. I must provide their parents with the same map so they will trust me with their children. Nevertheless, the challenge of communicating what lies ahead proves difficult for me every year.

Most teachers dread writing their introduction letter much like they dread Back-to-School night. The letter is necessary, but does not fully capture who you are as a teacher. You must set down in writing who you are and what your class is about in a one-page letter. This is your first impression on students' parents and you want to make a good impression; perhaps this is why teachers are so nervous about the task.

Writing Your Letter

Because this introductory letter is your first chance to connect with parents, you will want to be sure that the letter includes information that reassures parents that you are qualified, motivated, and organized.

With the passing of the *No Child Left Behind* federal law, it is becoming increasingly important for teachers to be "highly qualified" for their positions. The beginning of your letter needs to explain to parents how you became qualified for your teaching position. Begin by explaining where you earned your degree, what your major was, where you earned your teaching credential, and where you've had previous teaching experience. If you have completed postgraduate work, be sure to include this information, as well as any special training you may have gone through.

If you are just beginning your teaching career, this may be more difficult to accomplish. You may still be working toward your credential, without previous professional experience. My first job was as an intern. I had yet to earn my teaching credential and the only other teaching experience I had was observing classrooms and tutoring. I included these as my experience.

Approach this first paragraph as if it were a resume. Use strong verbs, describe experiences with wording that emphasizes your experience with teaching, and include work-in-progress if you are still working toward your credential. If you are a veteran teacher, don't include all your experience. Include only those experiences that make you "highly qualified" for your position.

Next you want to explain expectations for your classroom. You will want to reassure parents you are aware of the national and state standards. Also, if you are in a state where standardized testing is a measure of your school's performance, you will want to mention that you are working toward preparing all students for success on this assessment.

Next, you will want to give some general guidelines for your classroom, such as homework, absence, and behavioral policies. Be sure to keep this information general, especially if you are a new teacher. If you want to change any of your policies later, and you have written home about a policy, it will require a letter home explaining the change.

Finally, you will want to explain to parents how they can reach you. Give them the school's number, your e-mail address, and Web page address. Reassure parents about your intentions of ensuring every child's success, making it clear that you are eager to work with them and their children.

Many teachers require a parent signature on the letter to indicate that the parent has seen and read the letter. This is a good policy because you can then file the parent signature. If there is a dispute later about your expectations, you can gently remind parents that you communicated with them at the beginning of the year, hoping to avoid misunderstandings. This will move the conversation away from a blame game and into a situation of problem solving.

A sample letter might look like this:

Date _____

Dear Parents or Guardians,

Welcome to the new school year and my classroom. I am looking forward to a successful year with your child and want to assure you that I am prepared for a wonderful experience.

I hold a Bachelor of Arts in English from the University of California, Riverside, where I also earned my teaching credential. I also have done postgraduate work in Education Administration and English Composition. I have participated in many professional trainings, most notably the Inland Empire Writing Project and as a Language Arts Consultant for California Language Arts Project. I have been teaching for over 15 years.

My goal this year is to help your child build on the skills and knowledge attained last year and to extend those successes to future success. I will work diligently to be sure that all students in my classroom master the grade-level standards. Student work will often have a reference to which standard the work is aimed at. If you are interested in viewing the standards for this grade level, feel free to contact me or visit www.ca.edu.standards.

My classroom policies are very simple. Students have homework every night. If a child explains that he or she has already finished the homework, the child should be reading for pleasure for at least 20 minutes. My classroom expectation for students is that each student does his or her best work. I am available for extra help before and after school to ensure that every child is successful. If your child is going to be absent for an extended amount of time, please contact me so we can prepare the child for his or her return to the classroom.

It is important to me that we work together to ensure your child's success. Please feel free to contact me before or after school or by e-mail. I will do my best to respond within 24 hours.

Sincerely,

Ms. Mierzwik

E-mail/phone number

― ―

I have read and understand the policies outlined in the above letter.

_____
Student Signature

_____
Parent Signature

This letter may not win any awards for style, but it gets the job done. You have introduced yourself, given parents a general idea of how the class will work, and invited parents to contact you.

A letter my colleague uses looks like this:

Parents,

Welcome to a new year. My name is Ms. Huffs and I am very excited about the new school year and teaching your child. I know that this year will be a very successful and challenging year for all!

I have taught in Ontario/Montclair for 13 years and have been employed by Beaumont for the last 6 years. I love teaching and I know that all children will learn, achieve, and feel successful in my classroom.

Please read the following rules and policies with your child.

Classroom Rules

1. Respect yourself and others.
2. Raise your hand to speak.
3. Do not interrupt or disturb others who are working.
4. Follow directions.

Discipline/Consequences

I have a color chart in the classroom which is used for discipline. All students begin each day on green and colors are changed according to behavior.

Green = Excellent

Blue = Warning

Orange = Loss of recess

Red = Lunch detention

Excessive Problems = Principal referral and/or telephone call home

Students' behavior grades are based on how many times they change a color on the behavior chart. All students are given 10 points each week and 1 point is deducted for each time a color is changed.

Homework

Students will be given a school planner and be expected to record their homework assignments each day. This is so parents may check assignments if necessary. Students will then be responsible for taking their work home, completing their work, and returning it every day. Homework credit will be given for homework that is completed and returned on time. Credit will not be given for late work unless there is an absence or emergency.

Book Report/Reading Log

Each student will also be responsible for completing a book report and a reading log each week. These will be due on Fridays.

Progress Reports

Following the first few weeks of school, after students have had a chance to familiarize themselves to the assignments and the requirements in my classroom, I will be sending home weekly progress reports. These will show how your child is doing both academically and behaviorally in my class. These letters will be sent home every Monday or Tuesday, showing the previous week's work. These will need to be signed and returned the following day.

I look forward to an exciting year. Please feel free to contact me at anytime.

Ms. Huffs

Please sign, detach, and return the bottom portion

Student   Name   _____

Behavior Plan Acknowledgment:

I have received and reviewed the Classroom Behavior Plan with my child.

Parent/Guardian Signature _____

Date _____

Comments/Questions:

This letter is more detailed, which may be comforting to parents of younger students who are nervous about how their child will adjust to a new grade.

Both letters accomplish the same goals. It is important to craft your letter to reflect your expectations, and to reassure the parents you are there to help their children have a successful year.

Preparing to Send the Letter Home

This letter is a parent's first impression of you. It is important that you put your best foot forward with this effort. You want the letter to look professional, to be well written, and to make parents feel comfortable.

First, you will want to produce the letter on either the school's letterhead, or create a letterhead for your classroom. Most word processing programs have templates that will help you to create a letterhead for your classroom. The nice thing about a class letterhead is it helps parents keep informative letters from the school or the district separate from the letters they receive from you by a simple glance at the letterhead. The few minutes it takes you to create a letterhead will pay off all year because you can use the letterhead for all your correspondence with parents.

Next, you will want to ask someone to proofread your letter. Ask another teacher on campus or one of the school secretaries to proofread your letter. This can be intimidating, especially if you are self-conscious about your writing, but better a colleague or secretary catch any errors you've made than a parent. I have had letters returned to me with red marks all over them from a parent who disapproved of my use of English. As an English teacher, this is difficult to rebound from.

Finally, when you make copies for your parents, be sure the copies are clean and straight. The school will probably supply your paper, but if you can, get some better quality paper for the letter. Handing out a professional quality letter to your students to take home to their parents will impress both your students and their parents.

Your introductory letter home is the first impression you make on your students' parents. You want to assure parents that you are qualified, prepared, and available to them for a successful year.

Things to Remember

- Your letter should include your experience, expectations, and availability
- Treat your experience as if you were writing a resume
- Keep your expectations general, referring to grade-level standards
- Include how to contact you if there is a problem
- Have someone proofread your letter
- Print on quality paper if possible

8

Learning About Your Students From Their Parents

I met Dustin's mom in the counselor's office. It was November and Dustin was being transferred to my English class. He was in a class that had a teacher who quit abruptly and then had a series of substitute teachers.

As I entered the office, Steve, the counselor, rose to greet me. He introduced me to Dustin's mom. We shook hands and I sat in the student chair beside her. Steve had already told me why Dustin was transferring into my class, but he went over the details again. When he was done, I turned to Dustin's mom and said, "What can you tell me about Dustin? Does he like English? Does he like school?"

Dustin's mom stared at me blankly for a few beats then smiled. "No teacher has ever asked me about Dustin."

She went on to explain what Dustin's strengths and weaknesses were, what motivated him, and what he liked to do on his free time. Then she finished by telling me she was excited to have Dustin in my class.

Technically, Dustin wasn't even in my class yet. I hadn't met him and he had yet to bring home any assignments from me. I hadn't explained any of my policies or classroom expectations. Still this parent was excited to have me as her child's teacher.

As you can imagine, Dustin's parents were always supportive of everything that happened in class. Was Dustin a shining star because he transferred into my class? No. He was an average student who sometimes forgot his homework or failed to study and, thus, failed an occasional quiz or test. But I never had any discipline problems with Dustin, nor did I have to spend any time returning phone calls to his parents because they were unhappy about something in my class.

Using a Parent Survey

After my experience with Dustin's mom, I wished I could meet with every child's parents to interview them. I knew that was impossible so the following year I used a document that allowed me to gather information about my students quickly, while also winning the support of the students' parents in the first week of school. I now send this home with students on the first day of school, requesting that students return it to me by the end of the week.

Dear Parent or Guardian,

I have just met your child today. I want very much to have a successful year and would appreciate your help in starting the year off in the right direction. For me to best meet the needs of your child, it is important that I know as much as possible about him or her as it applies to school. Please fill out the following document with your observations. If you need more space, feel free to write on the back or on another sheet of paper.

Thank You,

Diane Mierzwik

English

Phone number

Your Child as a Learner

Name _____   Date _____

Grade _____   Class _____

Please indicate your observation of your child's learning behaviors in the following areas. Please provide explanations or examples where appropriate.

My Child	*Yes/No*	*Comments/ Examples*
1. Makes responsible choices about:		
• Listening (music, radio, conversation)		
• Reading (books, magazines, newspapers)		
• Viewing (TV, movies, posters, catalogs)		
• Playing (video games, PC games)		

2. Voluntarily shares his/her:		
• Drawing		
• Writing		
• Talking		
• Creative projects		
3. Expresses ideas:		
• In an understandable way		
• In an appropriate way		
4. Expresses opinions about:		
• Reading		
• TV programs, movies		
• Ideas presented at school		
5. Independently seeks information		
6. Persists in tasks		
7. Voluntarily engages in:		
• Reading		
• Writing		
• Problem solving		
8. Appears confident about learning		
9. Learns from errors		
10. Likes to read about. . . .		
11. Likes to write about . . .		

If there is any additional information that you think might help me to better know your child as a student, please feel free to write on the back of this page or another paper.

Thank you for your help. I look forward to working with you this year.

SOURCE: Adapted from *Frameworks*. Copyright 1993 by Illawarra Technology Corporation. Reproduced with permission from Wayne-Finger Lakes BOCES.

Students file the paper away with all the other papers they receive that first day to have their parents read over and sign. Then I begin collecting the papers the following day of class.

Because I teach older students, sometime during the first week of school (see Appendix), I also have students fill out a form similar to the one I send home. I give them class time as I take roll and handle any administrative problems that occur the first day of school: students not on my roll, students' questions, and so on.

The responses I get from students and parents vary, from simple checks to long narratives. In either case, I staple the forms together and read through them both. I find out a great deal about my students right away from these forms, such as: Does the parent see the child as the child sees himself? Is the child engaged in school? Is there history of a poor experience which has lead to low self-confidence in school? Generally, the responses from the parent and the child indicate to me so much about what has happened before this child came to be in my class.

Using Parent Letters

Another way teachers get feedback right away from parents is by simply requesting a letter. A fourth-grade teacher I know uses this technique every year and gets invaluable insight from the parents about her students for the year. She likes the letter because the parent is able to set the tone for the information.

The letter should ask for specific information pertaining to the goals of your classroom. If the parent believes that there is more you need to know, believe me, they will not hesitate to include that information. A sample letter might look like this:

Date _____

Dear Parent of Guardian,

I'm very enthusiastic about working with your child this year. I have an exciting school year planned and look forward to watching each of my students grow and learn during their time with me.

It would help me to know about your child from your perspective. You are in the unique position of observing your child outside the school situation and can give me many insights into their habits and behaviors, likes and dislikes, and interests. With this information, I will be able to manage, monitor, and adjust the curriculum to be sure it is meeting the needs of your child. Success breeds success and I want your child to be successful in my class.

Please spend a few minutes writing a letter explaining to me your child's homework habits, interests in school and out of school, how your child has done in school in the past, and any techniques used by previous teachers that were successful with your child.

If you have any questions, please feel free to contact me.

Sincerely,

Diane Mierzwik

Phone number

The letter allows parents more freedom in their response to you and may be easier for you to read.

I prefer the checklist/graph because it is easy enough for busy or overwhelmed parents to quickly go through the checklist while still allowing ambitious parents to write narratives about their child. Imagine how intimidating it could be for some parents to write a letter to their child's teacher.

In either case, what you have accomplished in the first week of school is to gather parent input about students. In doing this, not only have you got a head start on building a relationship with your students, but you have also set the tone for the parents. You have let them know that you are interested in their input and that you see their child's success in school as a team effort involving yourself, the student, and the parent.

Things to Remember

- The parent's view of his or her child is important to your relationship with the child
- Parents see your relationship as a partnership when they are included early in the year
- Be sure to ask specific questions to help guide parent input
- Request parent input the first week of school

9

Presenting at Back-to-School Night

Why is it that we are able to stand in front of our students all day, every day, but when faced with standing in front of a group of adults, namely our students' parents, sweat breaks out on our forehead, on our upper-lip, and under our arms? The thought of Back-to-School Night makes most teachers uneasy.

Back-to-School Night is often your first opportunity to meet parents, parents with whom you will want to build a relationship over the course of the year to ensure the success of every one of your students. It is important to make a good first impression. This is not very difficult to accomplish.

Making a good first impression simply takes a little organization and a deep breath. Everything will go smoothly if you keep the following in mind: Parents are your partners; it is your job is to reassure them that you want their help and that you are willing to help them to find the best way to make their children successful.

Preparing for Parents

Before Back-to-School Night you will want to be sure that you have made the proper preparations so that if you are a nervous wreck during your presentation, you will have organization on your side. When I was a new teacher, I made sure I had copies of all the texts out on the tables, examples of student work on the walls, handouts prepared, and a list of topics to be covered—speech notes—in my hands. That way I could fill up my time by directing the parents' attention to something other than how nervous I was. After teaching for many years, you will still make these preparations, but you will find you have so many things to share with your parents, that you run out of time rather than have the dreaded extra time.

The first thing you will want to do is to have textbooks available for the parents to peruse during the visit. This gives parents the opportunity to become familiar with the texts so they will be better prepared to support their child when work is sent home.

You will also want to make sure your classroom is attractive. If you are like me, your classroom is always attractive at the beginning of the year before things have had a chance to accumulate without a home. But you will also want to pay attention to details that make your room inviting for children.

If Back-to-School Night takes place before school starts, you should fill wall space with attractive bulletin boards that are appropriate to your curriculum. A "Getting to Know the Teacher" bulletin board, mentioned later in this chapter, is a great idea because it allows parents to find out about you. We all feel more comfortable with people we know something about. A parent who knows where you attended college or who knows you have children or dogs may be more apt to approach you because he also went to that college or has a dog. Anything that fosters communication between you and a parent is worth your time.

Providing parents handouts is a good idea. The handouts should be in addition to letters sent home with students because not all parents will attend this event. Providing a syllabus or a list of important dates for the class is always a good idea. I have also provided recent articles about homework time or fostering good readers. You are the expert in education and it is acceptable for you to provide information to parents about how to foster better study habits at home.

Finally, you will want to set up a sign-in area. Some schools provide sign-in sheets for parents and some don't. A simple sheet of paper where parents can sign their names, list the names of their children, and perhaps indicate a good contact time is a smart idea. A sign-in sheet could look like the one on the next page.

The sign-in sheet provides you with a record of who attended the event for future reference.

Organizing Your Presentation

Once you have your room in order and props for the evening organized, it is time to tackle what you want to say to parents. Organizing your "speech" helps to keep you on task and prevents you from forgetting to tell parents something vital to your class. An added benefit is that the structure will help to calm your nerves.

Your qualifications as a teacher are the best place to begin. This assures the parents that you are capable. You will want to include information such as the following: where you attended university and which degrees you hold, including where you earned your teaching credential; what previous experience you have had working in the school system; and any ongoing training you are involved in. As a new teacher you will want to be sure to share any experiences you have working with children, including the student teaching and fieldwork you completed as part of your degree program. You want parents to feel confident in your abilities to teach their children.

Parent Sign-in

Name _____ Child _____ Good Contact Time _____

1.

2.

3.

4.

5.

6.

7.

8.

9.

10.

11.

12.

Next it is a good idea to review standards and curriculum. A copy of the national standards for your grade level is an excellent handout for parents as well as a list of the textbooks and supplemental materials you will be using in class. If your district has a curriculum map, this is also an excellent handout for parents. These handouts provide parents with a guide to their child's school year. The more information parents have about your goals, the easier it is for them to support you.

After providing parents with the curricular goals for the class, it is a good idea to give several examples of clear expectations for assignments. For instance, I explain my homework policy so parents are aware that their children have assigned homework Monday through Thursday and may have homework on the weekends if they fall behind in class. I also provide examples of the type of homework and my expectations for proper completion of the homework. If the parents understand your expectations for the work, they will be able to support you in your expectations.

Many teachers use this time to go over classroom rules, expectations, and consequences. I choose not to do this because I believe that if I am an effective classroom manager, this is not necessary. I begin the school year expecting that every child is going to behave like an angel, and when a problem presents itself, I handle it on a case-by-case basis. Talking about consequences for poor behavior may give parents the impression that you are already anticipating problems.

Finally, end by assuring parents that you are approachable and willing to make accommodations for each child to ensure his or her success. Let parents know when is the best time to contact you, encouraging them to call for any reason. Parents want to leave feeling you are committed to having a successful year.

A second-grade teacher I know always ends her presentation with the reminder for parents that she may make mistakes but has every child's best interest at heart. She tells me that this one simple sentence has reduced the number of confrontations with parents to almost none in the last few years.

There will be parents with questions after your presentation. If you can, end the session by inviting parents to approach you with their questions. This works better than trying to answer specific questions parents have which may not apply to all parents. Back-to-School Night is not designed for conferencing about specific students, still you will have parents wanting to talk to you about their children. If the answer is long or difficult, politely explain that the issue is complicated and you would prefer to discuss it when you can give the issue your full attention. Pick-up the sign-in sheet and star the parent's name and assure her you will contact her during the week to set up an appointment.

If you have more than one session to conduct, remind parents of the time so that they may move on to the next session if need be, or make room for your next group.

Back-to-School Night is a wonderful time for you to present yourself to parents in a professional, caring manner. It provides you with an opportunity to gain parental support and lay the groundwork for a successful year.

Things to Remember

- Be prepared with textbooks, handouts, and an orderly room
- Prepare note cards to guide your "speech"
- Assure parents of your commitment to the success of every child in your class
- Invite parents to contact you regarding any matter

10

Requesting Parent Suggestions

I was attending a parent-teacher conference. All of the student's teachers were invited and so I was prepared for a round robin sharing of how the student was doing in class followed by a game plan of what we could all do to help the child be more successful in the future. What I got was an airing out by the parent in front of my colleagues about my classroom and curricular practices. At the time, I grew defensive, which is natural when attacked unexpectedly. Another colleague came to my defense, which helped to defuse the situation. All I could think at the time was "get this student out of my class."

It is difficult to have a child in class if you feel unsupported by the child's parents. That is one major reason it is important that you build a relationship with each of your student's parents. Without their support you will feel powerless with their child and apprehensive about contacting them when a problem arises. There were times early in my career when my response to this situation was to challenge the parents to transfer their child to another teacher. If you teach in a small district, this is not an option. If you teach in a large district and have this option, it can feel empowering to have the attitude, "lump it or leave it." Unfortunately, it is not very professional behavior.

At the end of the conference, the counselor in charge of the meeting asked me what I thought. I shared my reservations about teaching a child whose mother did not trust my ability, but I felt I got along well with the student and that he was making good progress in my class. She shared that the student had been to see her regarding other situations and enjoyed my class, so she was reluctant to transfer him out. We decided to leave the student in my class.

When I got home that evening, I contemplated how I was going to deal with a student in my class when I knew his mother thought I wasn't doing a good job. I went over in my mind her accusations, picking them apart for how she was wrong to question the job I was doing. I tried to convince myself that she was uneducated and mean-spirited and I had nothing to worry about; I was a great teacher. But there was a little voice inside of me that kept asking if this mother had any valid points.

Of course she did. As hard as it was to admit, she had brought up some flaws in my policies which needed to be addressed. For instance, when grading vocabulary sentences, I would only read for correct usage of the word, not grade on punctuation. She wondered what sort of standard I was setting for her child if he could get full credit for ten sentences, none of which had periods at the end. Grading these sentences for punctuation and usage would mean more time on my part, but I knew in my heart if I was going to assign this work, I owed it to my students to correct this work with diligence.

I had to decide if the time it took for me to grade this work properly was worth what I'd have to give up with my students in some other area, or if I needed to adjust the assignment altogether. Notice, I did not simply change my procedure to meet the demands of the parent, but I reflected on my practice to decide how best to use my time to give the most to my students.

This wasn't the only time I was confronted by a parent, and it still happens today. The difference is that now when I'm confronted by a parent, I do not grow defensive; I grow reflective. Plus, today I try to prevent attacks by keeping the communication between myself and parents open. One way I do this is by sending home parent surveys for how they perceive things are going for their child in my class.

Documenting Classroom Procedures and Expectations

In the first two weeks of class, after students have a general idea of the procedures of class, I send home a letter explaining all of my classroom procedures, including homework, grading, and classroom management policies. I require a signature on the letter so I am sure the parent has read the procedures and has a general idea of how the class will run. Many teachers include this in their introductory letter, as is documented with the second example in Chapter 7. This allows you to only send one document home. Waiting a few weeks before sending home a letter with expectations helps the child fully understand your classroom procedures so that if the letter is vague or unclear, the student has experience with you to clarify the letter for parents.

The letter could look like the one on the following page.

Notice that the letter does not give any specific information regarding consequences, grading procedures, or expected homework completion. This is in case you decide to change a policy during the school year. If you

Dear Parent and Student,

Welcome to week three of Ms. Mierzwik's class. To make this year a success, it is important that every student be held to high expectations. I want my expectations to be very clear.

I expect every student to be prepared for class each day with the proper supplies, including writing utensils, paper, and the proper books. It helps if students have a notebook for class and a backpack to carry all belongings.

I will be assigning homework Monday through Thursday. If a student feels that he or she has no homework, the student should spend time reading for the assigned book report or future projects. Occasionally, a student may have to work on a project over the weekend if he or she has not been able to budget weekday time accordingly.

If a student is absent, the child has the number of days absent upon returning to complete all make-up work. I would strongly urge that for an extended absence I be contacted for missed work so the student does not feel overwhelmed.

Late work is accepted for partial credit if turned in within a week of the due date. Work turned in later than a week will be accepted only on a case-by-case basis.

Adherence to classroom behavioral expectations is expected from all students. When a child has a difficult day, time-out in another classroom may be used along with a parent notification. If the problem persists other consequences will follow.

Grades are based on the child's ability to meet the grade-level standards as evidenced by classwork, homework, assessments, and teacher evaluations of performance in class. I will do my best to keep you informed of your child's progress.

I am looking forward to working with each student and anticipating another successful year. If you have any questions, please feel free to contact me.

Sincerely,

Ms. Mierzwik

have written a letter to parents stating a specific policy and then decide to change the policy, you will need to write another letter explaining the change in policy so there is no confusion. The purpose of the letter is to indicate to parents and students that you have a structure for the class and will follow through with that structure, not to detail how you will handle every situation that arises.

Those teachers who have more experience can add more detailed explanations of their policies because experience has proven the policy to be beneficial to teacher and student. For example, I include in my letter that every student must have a personal reading book for class. This is a policy that I have been using for over eight years. I know it works and there have been no objections to this requirement. Ms. Huffs in Chapter 7 includes her discipline system for behavior in her letter because she is an experienced teacher who has used the system for years. Be sure that if you include specific requirements, you are willing to stick to them for the whole year, or willing to inform parents of changes. You will look unprofessional if in your letter home you state a requirement that you fail to follow or decide to change midyear.

Clarifying Procedures After a Few Weeks

As a teacher, it is important to understand that reading a letter about the expected classroom experience and then having your child experience the class can be two very different things. You will find it useful to follow up a few weeks later with a letter home clarifying classroom procedures.

The purpose of the three-week letter is to verify with the parent whether the child and parent understand classroom procedures and can conform to those procedures or need accommodations. At this point, you probably haven't accomplished any large projects or any complicated units. You are still getting down procedures and laying the groundwork for the rest of the year. This is a perfect time to communicate with parents for a variety of reasons.

First, you let parents know that you want their input on how things are going with their child to ensure the child's success. For instance, even though you may believe the homework is self-explanatory, you may have a student who is struggling with the homework completion and a parent who is unsure how to help. Finding this out early prevents the child from giving up, the parent from growing frustrated, and you from forming an assumption about the child who is not turning her work in. Right away, you reexplain the homework policy, or make adjustments as necessary for the child.

Second, you send the message that you are willing to make accommodations to fit the needs of the child and the desires of the parents to ensure that the child is successful in your class. I had a parent who objected to one of the required readings for my class. Unfortunately, she waited until we were partially done with the novel before telling me. She didn't realize she would object until this far because I hadn't communicated with parents about the novel assuming that because it was district adopted, it was a good choice for all my students. At first I was offended, believing the mother felt I didn't have her child's best interest at heart. But after meeting with her, I understood that as a parent she was ultimately responsible for what her child was exposed to and it was my job as the teacher to support her in her decisions for her child. Together we found an alternative book that met both our goals for her son.

Finally, you begin a dialogue with parents about their child and their child's education so that you are both working toward the success of the child. Remember, you have already sent home a survey asking for parental input about the child as a learner. This further confirms that the parent is the child's biggest influence and that you need his or her help to make the most out of the time you have with the child in your class.

The three-week letter home should ask basic questions concerning classroom procedures, classroom expectations, homework completion, and the child's perception of the class. It could look like this:

Dear Parent,

As we reach the end of the third week of class, I wanted to check in with you about your child's progress in my class. As you know, I feel it is very important that we work together to ensure the success of your child, which requires that we communicate openly and frequently about how things are progressing. I want to remind you of a few things about class and then would like your feedback regarding how these things are affecting your child.

Please remember that I hold every child to the highest expectations in class, but am willing to make accommodations to help to ensure that your child can do his or her best work. Homework is an important part of the curriculum. It helps your child practice skills, extend information, and create new knowledge. Finally, your child's perception of class is important to his or her motivation. I want your child to feel capable and valuable in class.

If you could take the time to fill out the bottom part of this letter, providing feedback when necessary, it would help me to be sure that your child is progressing successfully with the curriculum, expectations, and procedures of class. You may want to discuss this survey with your child. If there is a concern, please share that with me honestly. I will do my best to address your concern. Finally, if you would rather speak to me in person, feel free to call so that we can set up an appointment to meet.

Thank you for your continued support,

Ms. Mierzwik

- -

Child's Name _____

1. My child feels comfortable with the pace   yes / no
   of the class:

2. My child is able to complete the homework   yes / no
   with little or no help:

3. The time it takes my child to complete   yes / no
   homework is reasonable:

4. My child feels confident that he/she can   yes / no
   be successful in class:

If you answered no to any questions, please explain or provide a phone number and time to reach you.

This letter is very basic, but provides the parent a chance to approach you with any concerns before they become problems.

Surveying Parents at the End of Unit/Quarter

Later in the year, after you have completed larger projects or more complicated units, you will again want to extend this opportunity for parents to approach you. Good times for this are at the end of a grading period or term, or at the end of a large unit.

As a veteran teacher, I have learned how to prevent misunderstandings over expectations for complicated units. Clarifying my expectations to prevent misunderstanding has occurred by contemplating the feedback from parents regarding my procedures. Usually, this feedback has been provided after a child has had a difficult time with an assignment and the parent shares with me what has gone wrong. I am not saying that when a student fails a unit or project, it is the teacher's fault. I am saying that it is a teacher's responsibility to make sure everything is clear and reasonable for students.

When you send home a letter requesting suggestions for how to improve the course, keep in mind that you are the professional. Also keep in mind that parents are the experts on their children. You want to balance your professional knowledge with their personal knowledge to provide the best experience for every student. If you choose to send home requests for suggestions, you must do so with an open mind, realizing that the point is for you to reflect on your teaching practices to find where you can comfortably make improvements or revisions to what you are doing.

A letter for this purpose may look like this:

Dear Parent,

We have just completed first quarter. We had a successful quarter with completion of our *House on Mango Street* project, our first book report, and our end of the quarter assessments.

To help me plan for second quarter, I would like your perception of how things went. If you have suggestions for ways I could have made the quarter more successful for your child, I would like you to share these with me. I strive to make my class a positive experience for every child and your help in this endeavor is invaluable.

Please take a moment to complete the bottom survey and return it with your child. As with any time I ask for your input, if there are concerns, feel free to explain them here, to leave a phone number and time I can reach you, or to call the school to set up a time we can meet to discuss your concerns.

I know that with your continued support, we can continue our success into the second quarter.

Thanks,

Ms. Mierzwik

Child's Name _____

1. The homework load was reasonable: yes / no

2. The homework extended or affirmed learning: yes / no

3. Directions for units and projects were clear: yes / no

4. Large assignments were organized so that   yes / no
   students were able to complete smaller units of
   the assignment before the final project was due:

5. My child feels capable in class: yes / no

6. My child feels able to ask for extra help in class: yes / no

7. My child had a successful quarter: yes / no

Please feel free to comment on any of the above or to contact me with any concerns. Thanks.

Obviously, you will want to include specifics regarding your class and expectations. Once again, this letter allows for parental input into what is happening with their child in your classroom. It sends the message that you are working together to ensure the child's success and that you respect the parent's input for what works best for his or her child.

Once you have collected these surveys from parents it is important to follow up with those who indicate a concern. Depending on the concern, you may need to call the parent as soon as possible to clarify a situation or simply to send a note home. Whichever approach you take, you must do something. If a parent fills out the survey with a concern and you do not respond, it sends the message that you aren't sincere about addressing his or her concerns.

Also, I always file these papers so I can refer back to them if another problem or concern arises. Having these papers on file can help you to reflect on the input a parent has given you before meeting with a parent. The papers can also serve to convince everyone involved that you are sincerely doing the best job you know how to do.

Sending home these types of requests for input can be daunting the first few times you do it. You must keep in mind that if you are sincere in your desire to include parents in a child's education—and every teacher should be sincere about this—then a parent's input should not be threatening, but enlightening. No teacher is a perfect teacher. All we can do is be sincere in our efforts to do our best. When a flaw or fault is pointed out, we must take the time to reflect on that input and then make some professional decisions about how to make sure everyone feels validated and successful in the situation.

You will be pleasantly surprised with how much positive feedback you receive. You'll find out which assignments and projects students and parents felt were worthwhile and successful. I've found out that the little girl who rarely speaks doesn't dislike my class but is rather shy. You'll find out that even though a child barely passed your class, he felt successful because of the support he received not only from you, but also from parents who were actively involved because of your communication with them.

These surveys provide you an opportunity to congratulate yourself on the students you are reaching and to contemplate what you can do differently to reach those students who may still be struggling.

Things to Remember

- Be specific when requesting suggestions
- View suggestions as a time for reflection
- Pay attention to the positive feedback as well as the negative
- Always respond to a parent who raises a concern
- Your professional viewpoint should compliment a parent's personal viewpoint

---

11

Conducting Parent-Teacher Conferences

Jacob was often off-task in class: forgetting his work, not having his books, and distracting those around him. When the time for parent-teacher conferences drew near, I was excited about gaining some insight into what motivated Jacob to choose his behaviors.

Jacob's mom appeared in my door with a cell phone to her ear and a briefcase in her hand. She had the slightly disheveled look of a woman with too many things going on, but holding it together nicely. She ended her phone conversation explaining that she was meeting Jacob's teacher, looking up at me with a smile.

Once the phone was put away, she reached out her hand and introduced herself. I directed her to my "conference" table and we settled in. I began by asking her how Jacob liked school. She sighed. Setting her jaw firmly she began explaining how Jacob felt the yard duties were picking on him, how this was a new school for Jacob and he didn't seem to be making the "right" friends.

I listened. I listened some more. Mom went on to explain that she had recently graduated from a rehabilitation program and Jacob had lived with his father while she was getting on her feet. Now she had a wonderful job which was demanding of her time, but provided well for her and her children. She wondered if the school couldn't react to Jacob in a more positive manner rather than always coming down on him so hard.

It would have been easy for me to explain that the wrath of the yard duties seemed to be well deserved, as was my own displeasure with Jacob and many of the choices he was making in class. I could have explained that beginning a new school was difficult enough without compounding that stress by being without his mother for the entire afternoon and most of the evening. I could have been very judgmental, except I have been in parent conferences—as a parent—when the teacher, principal, and support teachers all assumed that my child was acting out because my husband and I are bad parents.

No one is a perfect parent, just as no child is a perfect child. To conduct a conference looking for the parent to change dramatically his childrearing methods because a teacher thinks it would be best for the child is unrealistic. Teachers are not childrearing experts. (I thought I was until I actually had a child!)

When Jacob's mom finally turned from the space above my head she had been focusing on as she recounted what had been happening at home and focused on my eyes, I smiled. I offered to work with her to help Jacob feel more successful at school and for there to be better communication between the two of us to better support Jacob in his efforts. We came up with a plan which included my decreasing the workload until Jacob felt less overwhelmed and her checking Jacob's assignment sheet each night for homework and classwork completion.

The follow-through with this parent, as with many, was excellent the first few weeks and then it slowly declined. Luckily, it was enough to get Jacob back on track and to make Jacob aware that his mother and I both cared about him and would meet again to help him if necessary.

But I've also had conferences with parents straight from the pages of some poorly written horror novel. There were meetings with parents who were convinced that I did not have their children's best interest at heart, who believed I wasn't stimulating enough for their children, or who took it upon themselves to point out everything they perceived as faults in my teaching style. Sometimes these parents were teachers themselves, but usually they were not.

During these conferences, you must just grin and bear it, promise yourself you will not hold the parent's behavior against the child, and try to end the conference as soon as possible without being rude.

Usually conferencing is positive for all involved, especially if you are well-prepared, conduct yourself professionally, and show lots of empathy for parents and their efforts.

Preparing for Conferences

To prepare for a parent-teacher conference, it is important to have all of your documents in order. Be sure to gather your phone log of contacts, any written correspondence you have had with the parent, sample work from the student and perhaps a piece of sample work from an exemplary student (with the name removed), and your grade book or a grade print-out for the student if you are using a computer program.

Once you have gathered all of your documents, you will want to think about the student's strengths and areas in which you would like the student to improve. You'll want to think about your articulation of these strengths and weaknesses. Choosing the right words to express your concerns can make all the difference in the world.

A kindergarten teacher I know always begins the conference expressing how well the child is getting along with the other students. She says that most parents at that point are concerned that their children are making friends. She then goes on to discuss academics. My friend who teaches second grade begins conferences by explaining how well a student is reading and what progress the child has made with reading, because this is a major concern for parents of this age group. As children grow older, describing a child's strengths becomes much more specific to the child. One child may be very helpful in class whereas another is quite reserved but extremely studious. As the teacher, it is important to observe each child and be aware of the child's strengths, even if the strengths do not pertain to intelligence or ability in class.

Parents want to know that you like their child, that their child adds to the class, and that you see good things for the child's future. Expressing to a parent how a student brightens your day with his humor or her smile is enough to begin the conference on a good note. Thinking about these qualities will help you to articulate them at the meeting.

Next you will want to reflect on areas in which the student could grow. Even if the student is excelling in all areas, a parent wants to be reassured that you are doing your best to challenge the child. If a student is struggling in some areas, you will want to be able to explain specifically what seems to be causing the struggle. Having examples of the student's work helps many parents understand the struggle because they can see it evidenced in their child's work.

Finally, creating a plan to continue or further engage the student is important. If a student is struggling, having a plan for more structured lessons or for afterschool tutoring will reassure a parent that you are willing to provide extra assistance. If a student is excelling, a plan that extends the regular class lessons will give a parent confidence that you are striving to meet the needs of every student.

In addition to all of these preparations, if you are aware of any articles or books that you feel may expand a parent's knowledge of her child's situation, you will want to jot those titles down, or make copies of those articles. Many parents will nod politely; some parents will be enthusiastic about expanding their knowledge. In either case, you have shown that you have a broad base of knowledge about the subject.

Once you have thought about and written some notes on the progression of the conference, you will want to decide where you would like to conduct the conference. Many teachers set up an area that is neutral, away from the teacher's desk so a parent doesn't feel intimidated. A table in the classroom with some chairs pulled up to it seems to work the best. There are no distractions because only the paperwork pertinent to that conference is on the table. A neutral meeting area will put the parents at ease.

Meeting the Parents

When meeting parents, it is important to present yourself in a professional manner. Being on time, shaking hands, and introducing yourself (or greeting a parent you've already met and talked to) helps to set everyone at ease. Remember the sign-in sheet you used for Back-to-School Night? Use that to remind yourself if you met the parent that night and if so, greet the parent expressing how nice it is to see her again.

Direct the parent to the meeting area and begin the conference by asking the parent how she sees the school year progressing for her child. You may need to ask leading questions such as, "How is homework going?" "Is your child eager to come to school?" "Does your child seem interested in the things we're doing in class?" The answers to these questions will help you determine your tactics with the parent.

A parent who says all is well and her child loves school will want to be reassured that all is well and how you plan to make sure the remainder of the year continues to go well for the child. A parent who has concerns will need to be reassured that you are doing your best and that, with a united effort, the year can become a good one. Let the parent have time to express her impression of how things are going before sharing your impression.

There have been many times, especially with quieter students, when I have been nervous about whether I was meeting the needs of the child. It is always good to hear from the parent that the child is enjoying the class. There have also been times when I had no idea the child was not enjoying my class until a parent explained the situation to me. This information helped me as a teacher to examine my methods with that student.

Once the parent has expressed her impressions of how things are going, follow your plan by referring to your notes. Begin with the student's strengths, then discuss areas in which you would like to see improvement, and share your plan for bringing about a change for the student. During this time, allow for parent input and confirmations about your observations. Finish by confirming with the parent that the plan seems appropriate for the child. If necessary, you may want to schedule a follow-up meeting, phone call, or note home to be sure that things are going as planned.

End the meeting with a personal story about the student, something you observed the child do in class that was unique to the child. An anecdote about the child ends the conference on a personal note, reassuring the parent that you care about the child.

Recording Important Details After the Conference

If possible, directly after the conference, jot down some notes. Write down important aspects of your conversation with the parent so the next time you contact the parent you will be able to refresh your memory about your last meeting with him. Often it is not possible to complete this directly after the meeting, but it is important to do as soon as possible. Keeping a record of all your contacts with a parent is important to building a good relationship with the parent.

Finally, writing a quick thank-you note to the parent for her time is a great way to affirm the parent's commitment to her child's success at school. It also acknowledges your appreciation for the support the parent is providing for you. A thank-you note should also include a mention of the specific plan you and the parent agreed on for the child. This will remind the parent of her responsibility in the plan and confirm your commitment to the child.

Parent-teacher conferences can be nerve-wracking, but with the proper preparations, a plan for the child to be successful, a willingness to listen to a parent, and a clear picture of your goals for the child, this is a wonderful time to connect in a meaningful way with your students' parents.

Things to Remember

- Collect all records of contacts and correspondence with parent
- Collect samples of the student's work
- Take notes on positive attributes of the student
- Write down areas for improvement
- Create a plan for success for the child
- Designate a neutral area for the conference in your classroom
- Begin the meeting with a proper greeting
- Allow the parent to express her impression of how things are going
- Follow your preparations
- End the conference sharing an anecdote about the student

12

Thanking Parents

My first year teaching in Yucaipa, I had one student who was very "cool." He didn't socialize much with his classmates and seemed about five years more mature than the rest of them. He kept his distance and I respected that. I wasn't sure that I was doing anything worthwhile for the boy, but kept plugging along all year. At the end of the year, in my box I found a thank-you note from his mother. She explained to me how much her son had enjoyed my class, especially all the reflective writing we had done. She commented on how he had become very introspective and had grown from the exercise. She appreciated what I had done for her child. I was overwhelmed.

The note wasn't long and it wasn't on a very nice card. It was scribbled quickly on a piece of stationary found in almost anyone's house. I'll never forget that note.

Thank-you notes are a way for us to make connections with others. Think of the thank-you notes you have received and how much easier the note made your entire teaching day, not to mention working with that specific student. Weren't you more motivated to guide and motivate that student in particular, but also all students because someone had taken the time to express appreciation and gratitude for the tough job you do every day?

Parents also have a tough job and a thank-you note from you expressing how much you appreciate their involvement in their child's education can do plenty to cement a relationship you are building with a parent.

Thanking Parents for the Tough Job They Do

A friend of mine, Tracy, who teaches third grade, sends home with her students a "thank-you" for their parents the very first day. I have seen many different types of "thank-you's" and you might be familiar with a different one. If you choose to use this activity, you begin the year with parents who feel appreciated, motivated to help their children, and trusting of your care for their children.

Tracy puts the following items in a plastic bag that gets sent home with students: Smarties, a ruler, an eraser, play money, a party noise-maker, 100 Grand candy bar, and a gold medal with a note that says the following:

Gifts for Parents

- *Smarties.* Brain pills for the times when your brain is drained and you need to stimulate your mind
- *Ruler.* Because you all measure up to the task of providing for your children and being actively involved in their education
- *Eraser.* To remind ourselves and our children that we all make mistakes. When we make mistakes, they can be erased and we can be given a second chance
- *Money.* For how much we value our children and to remind us how much our children value us as parents
- *Party Noise-Maker.* To remember to celebrate all the successes, even the smallest successes
- *100 Grand.* For you and your invaluable contribution to your children
- *Gold Medal.* For your star performance as parents

This small gift sets the tone for parents. It allows parents the opportunity to reaffirm to themselves the important job they have in being a parent. It allows them to understand that you appreciate their job as parents. Finally, it gives you a chance to set the tone for your interactions with them for the entire year. Tracy has shared that after sending home the "gifts," when she finally does meet the parents, usually they begin by thanking her.

Sending Home Back-to-School Night Thank-You's

The first round of thank-you notes should be sent home to parents who actually attend Back-to-School Night. Most parents work, have other children, or are extremely busy in the evenings with dinner, church, sports, and other activities. For them to attend Back-to-School Night meant that they had to alter their schedule and make an effort to come meet you. Let's face it, your presentation probably wouldn't win any awards. You can't be blamed, you only had a few minutes in which to introduce yourself, describe your philosophy, give examples of curricular objectives, and give parents a chance to peruse the materials used in class. You had to do plenty in a little time. What Back-to-School Night does not allow you to do is meet parents in a meaningful way. A thank-you note allows you to make a meaningful connection with each and every parent who attends.

Thank-you notes can all say basically the same thing:

Dear _____ ,

I want to thank you for attending Back-to-School Night last Thursday. I know how busy parents are and making time in your schedule to attend shows me that you are very involved in your child's education. I wish I had had more time to speak to you individually. If you have any questions or concerns, please feel free to contact me.

Once again, thanks for your attendance.

Sincerely,

The note invites parents to contact you regarding any concern or questions they may have and acknowledges that you noticed they were in attendance. The easiest way to keep track of who attends is to have a sign-in sheet. The notes should be handwritten on either cheap stationary you bought at the local discount mart or on letterhead provided by the school. Try to spend three minutes each day writing one or two letters until you have written one for every parent in attendance. You probably will not hear back from any of these parents following the note and may conclude that it was a waste of time. That conclusion would be false. In actuality you have built a foundation of mutual appreciation for your roles in the students' success.

Reaching Uninvolved Parents

But the parents who showed up for Back-To-School Night are already involved. Sure, it's nice for them to feel you appreciate their involvement, but what about the parents who didn't come to Back-To-School Night? Those are the parents you need to get on your side. It's important to create opportunities for you to express thanks to these parents during the year.

One of the requirements of my class is that every student has a book he or she is reading for a book report. I take my class to the school library to allow them to choose a book, but the selection is very limited. Then I allow two days for students to find a book on their own by either visiting the public library or buying a book at the bookstore. Students must fill out a card which records the title of the book they are reading along with author, number of pages, and copyright date. Inevitably, on the day these cards are due, there are students who do not yet have a book.

I hear all the excuses, usually blaming the parent: "My mom was supposed to take me to the library." "My dad was supposed to take me to the bookstore." "My uncle has a book he wants me to read and hasn't given it to me yet." "This weekend." Then I wait. Each day, I call out the names of students who haven't filled out their card and those who are ready shuffle forward to complete the task. They always explain: "My Mom took me to the library even though she was suppose to be grocery shopping." "My Dad drove me to the bookstore last night at 8:45 because he knew it was important." "My uncle made a special trip to our house to bring the book by." These are all opportunities to be thankful.

Thanking parents for supporting your efforts in the classroom helps the parent feel that you are on his or her side.

Dear Mr. Jensen,

Joey explained to me in class today that you took him to the bookstore so he could buy a book to read for his book report. Thank you so much for helping Joey fulfill the requirements for my class. Your support will help him to be successful in class. The book he chose sounds interesting. I can't wait to read his report.

Sincerely,

Joey's Teacher

A thank-you letter needs to acknowledge how you knew the parent did something for the student. Usually this occurred because of a conversation you had with the student. It is good to mention this because it indicates that you have a relationship with the student. The letter needs to specifically state the action the parent took to help and how this action helps to support the child's efforts. Then try to end with a personal thought about the outcome of the project.

Following Parent Contacts With Thank-You Notes

Thank-you letters can also follow up phone conversations or conferences in which you and the parent discussed action to be taken to solve a problem. The thank-you letter will further motivate the parent to fulfill his or her end of the bargain.

This thank-you letter shows appreciation for a parent who is willing to work with you to help a child be more successful in class. It clearly states what the parent is to do at home after stating what steps you are taking in the class. It also invites the parent to contact you if the plan is not working. You would be surprised at how motivated parents are to keep their end of a plan going if they feel you are doing your best to implement your part of a plan.

Dear Mr. and Mrs. Fedro,

Thank you for taking time out of your busy day to discuss Samantha's education with me at the conference on Tuesday. I appreciate how we were able to set up a plan to help Samantha be more successful in my class. I will continue to work to help Samantha stay on-task during classroom time. I think that having you check her weekly progress report will help Samantha. If there is anything else you need from me, or if a modification of the plan is needed, please feel free to contact me.

Sincerely,

Samantha's Teacher

But, in all of these cases, the parent actually was involved somehow. How do you reach out to parents who are not involved? The parent has no phone, is a no-show for conferences, has not attended Back-to-School Night, and doesn't help his child with supplies or projects for school, for example.

It sounds amazing, but I have actually thanked parents for allowing their child to stay for detention.

A detention in my school is assigned by sending home a notice requiring a parent signature. The child returns the notice with the parent signature then stays after school for the assigned time. If you have been teaching for a long time, you have probably read the countless reasons a child can't stay after school for detention: no ride home, lessons after school, obligation to babysit younger siblings, or a parent just doesn't believe in detention. When I actually do receive a parent signature, I write a thank-you letter.

Dear Mr. Rouse,

Thank you for supporting me in my efforts to keep Albert on-task during class time. When Albert is focused in class, he is very successful and it is important to me that Albert is successful in class. He served his detention last Thursday. We spent the time working on some missing assignments and discussing ways for Albert to stay focused during class time. I appreciate your support in my efforts to make sure Albert has a productive year.

Sincerely,

Albert's Teacher

The parent may have just been happy that Albert wouldn't be in his hair for the afternoon, but your thank-you letter gave the parent the impression that his signature on the detention slip was a conscious decision to help Albert be a better student. The parent realizes that you are doing your best to help Albert and that you acknowledge the parent's support. A detention without a thank-you note can be perceived as just one more confirmation that Albert is a troublemaker and teachers don't like him. That is not the message you want to send home to a parent, however unintentionally.

Thank-you notes to parents take only a few minutes each day. However the support you gain from having parents feel appreciated for their efforts to help their child be successful in school will save you hours of frustration with parents who don't seem involved or supportive of your efforts.

Things to Remember

- Thank-you notes show appreciation for a parent's role in a student's success
- Keep the note simple
- Handwritten notes on stationary or letterhead is best
- Be sure to get the parent's name correct

13

Contacting Parents
Using E-mail

You would think that because I'm a teacher, I'm diligent about reading all the papers my son brings home from school. His notebook contains papers about flag football, the local tennis club, flyers for upcoming fundraisers, and flyers from his teacher about important dates. With all these papers to go through, I sometimes miss the flyer from his teacher.

If your students are older, parents are often reluctant to go through their child's backpack for papers. These older students, in between phone calls from their friends, their outside activities, and generally just being a kid often forget to give the papers to their parents.

I had one parent who requested I contact her each time I updated my grades. Her daughter had a habit of falling behind and this mother wanted to be sure that in between working, running a household, and driving her children to their activities she was supporting her daughter in being responsible at school. Each time I updated my grades using my computer program, I would copy her daughter's grade report and mail it to her through e-mail. The grade report listed the assignments, the grades for each assignment—indicating which assignments hadn't been turned in—and a cumulative grade. This was much easier for me than writing the mother a note, which many parents request. It saved paper from printing out a grade report each time I updated. And I didn't have to rely on the student to give the update to the mother.

Because of my efforts and the mother's diligence with keeping her daughter on track, Barbara passed my class with a strong B and I received a hearty thank you from the mother for helping her help her daughter have a successful year.

Creating an E-mail Account

Hopefully, you have a computer in your classroom that is connected to the Internet, making this method of communication with parents extremely convenient. If not, it is still worth your effort to walk to your school's computer lab or office or to use your home computer to contact parents using e-mail. It's easier than you think.

If your school district has not already set up an e-mail account for you through their district system, it is easy for you to create a free e-mail account through several services. I am most familiar with Yahoo and Hotmail. Both services offer free e-mail accounts. A colleague of mine sets up a new e-mail account each year, canceling the previous year's account. This way he can avoid erasing all his old addresses and messages and just start fresh with the new group of parents and students. Both Yahoo and Hotmail allow you to do this.

If you choose to open an account with one of these services, you will want to use a name for the account that will make it obvious to parents where the e-mail is coming from. For instance, I name my e-mail accounts: Ms. M'sEnglish(year). This way when a parent checks her e-mail, she will see your e-mail address and know immediately the e-mail is from her child's teacher.

Once you have found the account provided by the district or set up an account on your own, you need to give parents the option of being contacted through their e-mail. A letter home giving parents your e-mail address and a request to send you a message if they would like to be able to receive messages from you via e-mail is the easiest way to offer this option. The letter might look like this:

Date _____

Dear Parents,

To ensure your child's success in my class this year, I feel very strongly about being able to communicate with you about important due dates and expectations. I also want to be available to you if you have any questions or concerns regarding your child, class projects and activities, or class expectations.

One way for us to communicate easily is through the use of e-mail. I realize that not every parent has e-mail and if you do not have e-mail, rest assured that I am always available through a phone call. For those parents who do have e-mail, if you would like to use this vehicle as a means to keep in contact with me, it is a very easy process to set up.

My e-mail address is _____ . If you would like me to use e-mail as a way to keep you informed, please e-mail me a message indicating this and I will be able to add your e-mail address to my address book. I will use e-mail to inform you of upcoming due dates and activities in class, as well as to inform you of any specific information I feel you need regarding your child.

I believe the success of your child in my class depends on a good working relationship between the school and family. Being able to communicate with you is very important to me. I hope that the use of e-mail will provide one more way for us to work together toward a productive year.

I look forward to e-mail messages from those of you who are able to take advantage of this technology, but once again want to assure parents who do not have this technology that I will be available in other ways for you.

Thank you,

Diane Mierzwik

After sending home this letter, all you have to do is check your e-mail for messages from parents indicating their desire to take advantage of your offer. Once you receive a message from a parent, you simple click *add to address book* and the e-mail server will create an address book with each parent's e-mail address. You may need to insert the parent's name and the name of the parent's child so you can remember which e-mail address goes with each parent. Very rarely does a person use their legal name for e-mail unless it's an account through their work.

Most e-mail servers provide within the address book an *Everyone* address. This is another advantage to setting up an account to use specifically for your classroom communications. Sometimes this is called a "list serve." Using this option makes it very easy for you to contact all your e-mail parents at once.

Each time you receive an e-mail from a parent indicating a desire that you keep him or her updated using e-mail, you need to respond with a message confirming you received the e-mail message and look forward to using e-mail for communication with the parent. A message could look like this:

Dear _____ ,

Thank you for contacting me via e-mail. I look forward to using this technology to keep you updated on your child's progress as well as important due dates and activities occurring in class.

If you ever have a question, please feel free to contact me using this account. I will be diligent about responding to e-mail and try to get back to you within 24 hours.

I look forward to a successful year with your child.

Sincerely,

This message does two things to establish your e-mail connection with your students' parents. First, it invites parents to contact you with any questions or concerns. Second, it begins the connection on a positive note. Beginning the communication with a positive message allows you and the parent to begin your relationship cooperating with one another.

Communicating With All Parents

Once you've established initial contact with a parent, whenever you create a document, especially those that describe assignments or list important dates in your classroom, you will have the ability to send it to all the parents on your e-mail list. Simply open "write" or "compose" and then paste the document into the text box and press "send." This is an easy and time-efficient way to keep parents informed. It is important to continue to pass out your handouts in class and to send flyers home with students, but your e-mail messages act as a backup to these forms of communication.

Be sure to save a copy of all these documents in your mail sent file which will record for you a copy of the document and who received the e-mail. This works as a handy list of parental contacts for future reference.

Contacting Parents Individually

Another beneficial use of e-mail is to contact parents individually. You can use this method of communication in several situations:

- You want to contact the parent immediately about a concern but cannot reach the parent by phone
- You want to share information with the parent without the student's knowledge
- You are unable to use snail mail to send good news, congratulations letters, thank-you letters, or invitations to visit

E-mail is very convenient because you access it when you have time and the same goes for the parent. If you feel uncomfortable calling a parent in the evening, late at night, or on the weekends, e-mail is very unobtrusive.

If you decide there is a concern you need to share with a parent and you cannot contact the parent by phone, using an e-mail message is an option. I want to caution though, when you contact a parent using e-mail, there is not an exchange of ideas about how to solve a concern. There is no voice inflection or body language to make it clear to the parent that you want to work with the parent to help a child be successful in your class. There are only words on a page which can be interpreted in a variety of ways. It is very important to choose your words carefully.

If you are e-mailing a parent with a concern, my suggestion is to only indicate that you need to speak with the parent, ask when it would be a convenient time to contact the parent by phone, and leave a phone number and times when a parent can contact you by phone. If you are resorting to e-mail because you haven't been able to contact a parent by phone, it is important to make yourself available outside of school hours and to even give the parent a home or cell phone number. It is fine to give certain hours it would be best to call, but make yourself available to the parent. An e-mail message of this sort might look like this:

Dear _____ ,

Today in class, _____ seemed distracted. To ensure his success, I would like to speak to you about the situation. I tried to contact you by phone (date and time) but (answering machine, voice message, busy signal, no answer).

I can be reached at school before and after school or during my conference period from _____ to _____ , or feel free to contact me at home. My number is _____ and the best time to reach me is between _____ . If these times are not convenient for you, please let me know when would be a good time to contact you.

In the past, _____ has done a good job in class and I want to be sure that he continues to be successful.

I look forward to speaking with you about this situation.

Thank you,

The use of the word "distracted" can encompass almost any concern you may have regarding a student. Distracted could mean that the child was off-task to the point of not turning in work; disruptive; or simply unprepared for class. But, "distracted" does not have harsh negative connotations. It implies that the behavior was an aberration and can be solved easily.

After sending this message, the parent's response will indicate to you how you should proceed. If the parent phones you, you will be able to discuss the situation with the parent. If a parent e-mails you requesting that you share the concern via e-mail, then follow those instructions. Be sure that when you e-mail a parent about a concern, you once again choose your words carefully.

E-mailing a parent with a concern can be a delicate situation. If there is a misunderstanding when you talk on the phone, it usually can be resolved by explaining the intentions behind your words. Nothing that happened is recorded. With an e-mail message, however, if your intentions are confused because of a poor choice of words, the e-mail can be printed and used against you.

Be sure to carefully draft an e-mail message regarding a concern. Avoid drafting if you are still upset or frustrated with the child. Before sending the e-mail, print a copy and have a colleague read it for an opinion on your choice of words. You want to be careful not to alienate the parent or put the parent on the defensive. Remember, you want the parent to support your efforts.

Begin e-mail messages with something positive about the student. It can be the student's behavior, a past success, their friendly demeanor, or anything that begins the message on a positive note. Then describe the concern, indicating that given the child's past behavior, you are surprised by the situation. Next, ask the parent if there is something that has confused the child or if there is something you should be sensitive about regarding the child. Many times when a student has suddenly become belligerent or uninvolved in class, there has been a disaster in the family. Having this information can make you much more sensitive to the situation, allowing you to adjust expectations while the child is going through the difficult situation. Finally, end the message with an invitation to contact you again. A message of this nature might look like this:

Dear _____ ,

_____ has (name a specific thing the child does well in class) received a 100% on homework thus far in the year. I was very concerned yesterday when she did not have her homework completed for the week. This is unlike her. I want to offer my help to solve any problem that prevented her from completing the homework.

Please let me know what I can do to help solve this situation. _____ is welcome to turn the assignment in late for partial credit unless there were some extenuating circumstances.

Sincerely,

The message, above all, needs to convince the parent that you are a reasonable person who expects the child to succeed and that you are willing to go above and beyond to ensure the child's success.

Sending a message regarding a behavioral issue requires some delicacy. You want the parent to understand that classroom expectations must be adhered to while also indicating that the student is capable of the expected behavior. A message concerning this type of problem might look like this:

Dear _____ ,

Thank you for responding to my e-mail. The concern I had about _____ was his behavior in class. Unfortunately, _____ chose to talk out of turn many times today. I repeatedly redirected his behavior, but I'm unsure if he understood how distracting he was for the other students and me.

_____ has been quiet and attentive in the past and I know that when he is motivated, he can act appropriately in class. If there is something I can do to help motivate him to make better choices during class time, I would be happy to do so. As it stands, if his behavior continues, he will be assigned a consequence.

I know that working together, we can help _____ be successful in school.

Let me know what I can do to help.

Sincerely,

This message begins by acknowledging the parent's involvement in ensuring the success of the child by responding to your message. It then goes on to specifically describe the behavior and what you did to try and solve the problem. It then points out that the child has behaved appropriately in the past and assures the parent that the child can improve the situation if he chooses to. It then places the responsibility on you to solve the problem if the parent believes that the situation is arising out of something you are doing, but indicates that if the behavior continues, the child will receive a consequence. The consequence is left vague on purpose. You want to gauge what the parent will support before assigning consequence. There is nothing worse than assigning a detention only to receive a note from the parent indicating that he refuses to allow his child to serve a detention. If you assign a consequence that is not supported by a parent, it puts you at odds with the parent and takes away any authority you had with the child. Finally, the message ends with the invitation to contact you with suggestions about how to solve the situation.

One of two things will happen after this message. The parent will e-mail you indicating either that there is something you need to be sensitive about or that the child is aware of the parent's support of your classroom rules. Or you will not hear back from the parent, but the child will improve immediately. In either case, the e-mail was well worth your effort.

E-mailing Grade Updates

The final reason to use e-mail is for those parents who request updates regarding their child. If a parent requests regular updates, you want to define specifically the scope and regularity of these updates. I have had parents, as mentioned, who requested that I send a copy of the child's grade report each time I updated grades. I have had parents request that I e-mail a weekly indicator of good behavior or responsible behavior regarding work turned in. Be sure to stay within this definition for the e-mail correspondence and if something unusual comes up, to contact the parent by phone first and then with a carefully worded message on e-mail. Do not assume that because you e-mail a parent frequently, that it gives you permission to use e-mail beyond the parameters of the relationship you previously established.

E-mail is a wonderful tool to contact parents who are very busy. It allows you and the parent the flexibility to contact one another when it is convenient. It allows for immediate communication between you and the parent. You will find that using e-mail to connect with parents is a wonderful use of technology.

Things to Remember

- Do not use slang or shortcuts when sending e-mail to parents
- Always write in a professional manner
- Be sure to address the parent correctly
- Always use spell check and proofread just as you would with any other professional document before you hit the send button
- Save all correspondence in a sent mail file for record keeping
- When e-mailing about a concern, use language aimed at solving the problem

---

14

Phoning Home

It was a Friday afternoon and I had tried several times over the course of the afternoon to contact Christina's parents to let them know Christina had improved since the last time we spoke. She had turned in all her homework for the week, had been attentive in class, and was generally making an effort to do well. Before I pushed away from my desk to begin the weekend, I tried one last time. The phone line was still busy. I quickly wrote down the number on a slip of paper and stuck it in my pocket, thinking I might call from home.

Friday evenings at my house are busy. The whole family is happy to be done with the regular schedule. We all are in limbo about meal plans because we usually go out. We are all exhausted and perfectly happy to sit in front of the television or with a book or game for a few hours. In the middle of all this I felt that slip of paper in my pocket. I wondered if I should bother Christina's family on the weekend.

I asked my husband what he thought. When he found out that I was calling with good news, he encouraged me to call. So what if I interrupted their evening? Good news is good news.

I dialed the number and reached Christina's dad. I explained who I was and why I was calling, reminding him of our phone conversation a few weeks ago. I apologized for interrupting his evening and shared that I only wanted to take a minute to let him know that I had noticed an improvement in Christina's classroom behavior and participation. I explained specifically that Christina had turned in all assignments and had been very attentive.

Christina's dad sighed. I had interrupted their evening, their evening of arguing. Christina had brought home an assignment sheet from another class showing some missing work. Her dad had been lecturing her about being responsible while Christina had been trying to convince her dad that she was trying harder. I happened to call in the middle of this. I explained that I didn't know what was happening in other classes, but Christina was definitely trying in my class. He thanked me for the phone call and explained that I had made a good weekend possible for his family. We hung up.

On Monday, Christina did not run up to thank me for calling home. She never even mentioned that I had saved her from her dad's lecture, but she was attentive and on-task that day. She was responsible with her work and was not disruptive once all week. She had already begun to make the changes necessary to be successful in my class. My phone call home reinforced her behavior and it continued for the remainder of the year.

As teachers, we are encouraged to call home when there's a problem with a student. The purpose of the phone call is to communicate with the parents and, hopefully, gain some support from home. We are rarely encouraged to call home with good news. I have never in my 16 years of teaching been told to call home with good news; however, it is one of the most productive activities I do.

I remember the first time my son's school called. I received a message in the classroom that his school had called and I spent the next 40 minutes (while waiting for a break to return the call) telling myself that it *wasn't* bad news. It was.

Parents understand that when a teacher calls home, something is up. I call home when something is up, good or bad, but there are ways to make all phone calls productive, and there are ways to make every phone call positive.

Calling for a Job Well Done

A great use of phone calls, but one that is easily overlooked is to call home with good news. My example with Christina and her father grew out of an earlier phone call to discuss a problem, but the same results can be accomplished by calling home whenever a child had done something good in class. It only takes a few minutes but everyone wins. You share unexpected good news with a family, making their day more pleasant. You reinforce the behavior or activity exhibited by the child. You establish the conviction for the parent that her child is and can be successful in school and that you are a teacher who values children who are successful.

Calling home is a wonderful way to immediately provide feedback for a child who did something that caught your attention during the day. Before you push away from your desk at the end of the afternoon, it only takes a few minutes to make the phone call, and you leave the day on a positive note.

There are a variety of positive things a teacher can call home about. Some of them are things already discussed such as completing homework and classwork or being attentive in class. Other things include when a child:

- Is kind to another child
- Asks a thoughtful or provocative question
- Does work that is exemplary for the child

- Is helpful to you or classmates
- Shares a skill or talent with you or the class
- Was funny

It is important to be very specific about what the child did to warrant your phone call home. Calling home to tell a parent his child is a delight is nice, but just like how you want to be specific when you are complimenting a child, you want to be specific when you call home. The reason for the call must be sincere to be valued.

A phone call may proceed like this:

Mr. Robins, this is Richard's teacher. I hope I'm not interrupting. I just wanted to share with you that today Richard did a wonderful thing. We have a new student in class and Richard volunteered to show the new boy around. He was very diligent, spending every recess with him and his lunch, even walking him to his bus. I know Richard made the new boy feel very welcome today. I was very proud of how kind Richard was.

Usually the parent will respond with surprise or a confirmation of the child's positive attributes and gratitude that you took the time to call.

A phone call about a student's work in class might proceed like this:

Ms. Davis, this is Kevin's teacher. I hope I'm not interrupting. I just wanted to share with you how proud I am of Kevin's book report. It's obvious he took extra time to complete the artwork and the way he organized his information was very creative. I'm so pleased with his progress in class and wanted you to know. I look forward to Kevin's future assignments.

Once again, the parent will tell you about how wonderful she thinks Kevin is, or how the book report motivated Kevin. The last sentence indicates that you are expecting this quality of work from Kevin in the future without putting pressure directly on Kevin. It raises the teacher expectations, which we all know raises student achievement.

A phone call home with good news is the fastest, easiest way to gain parental support. Later, that parent is going to be at the child's basketball practice, soccer game, or ballet rehearsal. When the other parents share the problems their children are having in school, this parent will share what a great job his child is doing—the teacher even called home to let him know. All the other parents will immediately want to know who that teacher is.

Calling Home to Avoid a Problem

It is important to call home when a student is having a problem in your classroom. First, the phone call alerts the parent to the problem before it grows out of hand. How many times have we been confronted with a large problem and thought that if we had only known about it sooner, it would have been much easier to solve? Second, the phone call alone may solve the problem. Students are aware when they are getting away with something in your class that wouldn't be allowed at home. Often as teachers we assume that a child behaves a certain way in class because he is allowed to behave like that at home. Sometimes this is true. Many times it is not. There have been many times when I have called home because of a student's behavior to have the behavior disappear the very next day. Finally, a student often knows when you are unwilling to make a phone call home, which encourages her to be sure to tell her side of the story to her parents without worrying about your side of the story. She may even say things to you like, "My mom doesn't think you're a good teacher." This can further intimidate you. Why call home when the parent already doesn't like you? You probably won't get any support anyway. If a student says this to you, it is important to call home that afternoon to clear up the confusion. I always say, "Well, I need to talk to your mother about that." Then I call home that afternoon.

Calling home can be intimidating, especially after a few "bad" phone calls home. Bad phone calls are the ones in which the parent makes excuses for the child or blames your failings as a teacher as the cause of the problem. I still remember the phone call I made to Jordan's mother. I explained Jordan was having trouble with appropriate behavior in class. The mother's response was "He doesn't have trouble in any other class. What are you doing wrong?" Of course, I spoke later to his other teachers, and they too had trouble with Jordan, but hadn't taken the time to call home. Needless to say, my motivation for calling parents dropped significantly after that phone conversation. And you will have those conversations, especially if you make the same mistakes I made during that phone call.

When I used to make phone calls home, I explained the problem and left it at that. Something along the lines of, "Jordan talks out of turn constantly and is disrupting class. I wanted you to know that if his behavior continues, he will be sent out of class and a discipline notice for the office will be written." No wonder the mother grew defensive. I stated there was a problem with her child and the choices for action included the student adhering to my rules or being kicked out of my class. When you call home with this attitude, the parent feels he is to blame for not raising his child right and that he needs to solve the problem for you.

If you are having problems with a student, you are partly to blame. Not because you are doing something wrong, but because you haven't figured out what to do right for that student. Calling home is an opportunity to find a solution with the parent.

One suggestion I have before making another phone call home is to call Microsoft technical support or American Online technical support. I've called both of these recently. Both phone calls were made while I was extremely frustrated and scared, scared that all my hard work on my computer had been lost. I was astounded by how good I felt when I hung up, although neither of them was able to solve my problem. But the people helping me told me over and over that they were going to work on a solution. The solution never came, but I was convinced that they had tried their best. When we call parents, that's what we want them to believe, that we are trying our best to find a solution.

A solution is what you are calling home for anyway, just be sure you are willing to be part of the solution. And be careful you don't sound like you have all the answers.

Before I had my own child, I often called home with a list of parenting techniques for a parent to implement so their child would come to school prepared to learn. Then I had my own child and learned to be more empathetic and to offer suggestions to parents, realizing that not all suggestions will work for all children. I remember one phone call when I simply listened to a mother talk about how she tried everything and still her son refused to do homework. I could have easily dismissed her frustration with a belief that if the boy was still not doing homework, there was no way she had tried everything, at least not correctly. Instead, I listened and then said, "I know it's hard. I have my own son. We just need to have faith that they'll land on their feet." Later that year, the boy did start doing his homework and the mother thanked me for being supportive.

Things to keep in mind when you are calling home searching for a solution to a problem:

- Call before your frustration level is too high
- Begin the call stating something positive about the child
- Explain the situation to the parents, indicating which interventions you have tried
- Ask if the child has talked about the situation at home and, if so, what the child's perception of the problem is
- Be ready to accept that your methods have not worked with the child
- Ask the parent if the child exhibits the same behavior at home and, if so, what works at home to curb the behavior
- Assure the parent that you will try the agreed-upon technique and are willing to make adjustments to ensure the success of her child
- Indicate if you feel the need to keep in touch or extend the invitation for the parent to contact you with any other concerns or suggestions

A phone call may proceed like this:

"Hello, this is your Sarah's teacher, Ms. Mierzwik. Is this a good time to talk?"

"Yes."

"Great. Sarah has been doing a great job with her in-class assignments. She is attentive and follows directions."

"Well, Sarah has always enjoyed school."

"I'm so glad. *We* are having a problem though with Sarah turning in her homework. She seems to be leaving it at home on a regular basis, or bringing it to school incomplete. *I wonder if there is something I could do to help get Sarah to get her homework done.* Has she shared this problem with you?"

"No, I had no idea she wasn't completing her homework. As a matter of fact, when I ask her about homework, she tells me she had none or that she completed it in class."

"Unfortunately, that's not the case. *Maybe Sarah is confused about the homework policy.* Let me explain to you how it works so you can help her get back on track. (Explain policy here). Does that make sense to you?"

"Yes, I will be sure to have a talk with Sarah about this and she will have her homework tomorrow."

"Thanks so much for your help. It's so important to me that Sarah is successful in my class. If you have any other questions or concerns, please call me. Would you like me to check in with you about Sarah's homework?"

"No, I think once I discuss this with Sarah everything will be solved. Thank you for calling."

"Thank you for your support."

The areas italicized are key phrases to prevent the parent from being on the defensive, and to help the parent to believe that you are searching for a solution together. Remember these key phrases:

- We are having a problem
- I wonder if there is something I can do to help
- Maybe _____ is confused

Others include:

- What works at home with _____
- Do we need to adjust the assignment for _____
- What can I do differently to help _____
- Thank you for your support

When you call home to solve a problem, keep that as your goal. Your goal should not be to get a child in trouble.

If a child improves after the phone call home, be sure to follow up with another phone call to share with the parents that you have seen improvements and appreciate the effort the child is making and the support the parent gave you.

Using Automated Phone Calls

One final use of the phone is to use your campus's automated phone calls. Many school campuses have this system and it is primarily used to contact parents with general messages about upcoming events or a child's absence, but it can easily be used by you for messages to your students' parents.

The automated system records a message and then the computer dials each number previously programmed. When the phone is answered, the recorded message plays for whoever answers the phone. Using the system requires that you set up on the computer which phone numbers to call and record a message to be played. If you use the system for messages that will benefit your entire class, it requires that you only need to set up the computer information once and save it. Then each time you have a message for home, you record the message and push play on the computer.

Each automated system is slightly different. Your best bet for using the system is to ask the secretary who uses the system for the school to help you set up a file for your class. Once the file for your class is set up, you can use it anytime during the school year. You may need to update the file for students who are added or dropped from your class during the year.

I have used the automated system to alert families of upcoming due dates, especially for long-term projects. I assign a book report at the beginning of each grading period, handing out the due date and requirements once students have chosen books to read. Even though I remind students often and the due date is posted in my classroom, someone always seems to forget. Calling home to remind families of the due date helps to prevent forgetfulness.

A recorded message may proceed like this:

Hello. This is Ms. Mierzwik, your child's English teacher. I am calling to remind you of the upcoming due date for your child's book report. The due date is Friday, May 5th. Your child should have a paper with the requirements for the report, but if there are any questions, please call me. Thank you.

I have had many parents thank me profusely for reminding them of due dates. I have had some students complain to me that my phone call meant they couldn't go to an activity until their report was done. That's a good thing in my opinion. The automated phone call helps me avoid handing out consequences for late work, helps the students' parents support their children in their responsibilities, and helps the students make school a priority. It is well worth the effort.

The answering machine is fine for positive phone calls, but you should never leave a negative message on an answering machine. If the answering machine picks up and you were calling about a concern, simply state who you are and leave a phone number and a time you can be reached. "I'm calling regarding _____ . My number is. . . . ." Make sure if there is a concern, you are speaking to a person when you share the concern.

When you call home, be sure you know the parent's name. Do not assume a parent has the same last name as the student you are calling

about. If you are unsure, refer to the parent as "The mother or father of
_____ ."

Keep a record of all phone calls, whether positive or negative. If you must contact the parent again, you will appear to be more professional if you have your contacts logged. Log the date, the purpose of the phone call, who you spoke to, and what the result was.

If the phone makes you uncomfortable, only use it for situations that need immediate attention.

Calling home only takes a few minutes of your time but can result in a connection between yourself and a student's parents that is worth hours of avoided frustration for you, the parent, and the student.

Things to Remember

- Always ask if it is a good time to talk
- Be sure you know the parent's last name
- Discuss specific behaviors you have observed, both positive and negative
- Keep a log of phone calls for your records (see resource for a sample phone log)

15

Mailing Home Good News Postcards

This year I had a student who enjoyed testing my limits. Interestingly, whenever I asked him if I should call home about his behavior, the behavior ceased. I decided to contact home, but with good news. Many studies have found that when contacting parents regarding good behavior, the behavior and achievement of that student improves (Barth, 1979). I wrote a good news postcard for the student emphasizing that he could follow directions when motivated. The parents sent me a long letter thanking me for the postcard, explaining that their son needed positive reinforcement and that my tactic was successful. The student still had his moments, but I knew he thought of himself in a positive manner in my class; his parents supported me; and, with gentle reminders, he was an excellent student the rest of the year.

One of my most successful ways of connecting with parents and students is to send home good news postcards. The idea grew out of my need to not let anything go to waste. Our photographer for school pictures each year provides postcards that read "Good news from YJHS (the initials of our campus name)." We receive stacks and stacks of these postcards. One of the secretaries places a few of them in our box and, until recently, the rest filled a drawer in the front office. The postcards I received in my box sat in my desk drawer for the longest time. I pushed them out of the way whenever I was searching for something. Finally I decided to send a few home.

The first few postcards I sent home were at the end of a grading period. I sent postcards to students who had the highest grade in the class. The postcard read:

> Dear Parents of _____
>
> I just wanted you to know that _____ received the highest grade in her class for this grading period. I am very proud of _____ and enjoy having her in class.
>
> Sincerely,

That started it for me. The response I got from the students motivated me. Most students would approach me when no one else was around and thank me for the card, explaining how proud their parents were of them. To see the joy on my students' faces because I took a few minutes to write a short note to their parents about something they had accomplished on their own motivated me to do it again.

I found that drawer in the front office and took a whole stack of cards. One of the secretaries stopped me, explaining she had already put some of those in my box. I smiled and told her I had more good news to share.

Using Postcards

My first postcards were sent to students' homes for academic achievement, but I soon began to send postcards to recognize good participation and behavior. I began to find reasons to send home postcards to every student in class. At first students would ask me discreetly if everyone in class received a postcard. I always answered, "Everyone who deserved one." Eventually, the students began to share with each other that they had received a post-card, and the students who hadn't received one asked me why. "To receive a postcard you have to do something extraordinary in my class." Students began to try to do something good to earn a postcard.

The postcards had an effect on my class I never dreamed of. Students understood through the postcards that I was aware of their accomplishments in my class. My postcard recognized the accomplishment or good behavior; the accomplishment or good behavior continued or even increased after I sent the postcards home. I even tracked student grades, focusing on completion of homework and classwork. The majority of the time student achievement increased after a postcard was sent home.

When I address a postcard, I always address it "Dear Parents Of _____" because this salutation acknowledges that the child is the focus of the postcard and emphasizes the relationship between child and parent. I then follow with a statement of why I am generally proud of the child, what specifically the child did, and how I'm looking forward to continued progress or success. A postcard might look like this:

Date _____ Dear Parents of _____ , I just wanted you to know how proud I am of _____ . This week _____ turned in all of her homework on time. It is so wonderful to see _____ acting responsibly about her work. I am looking forward to _____'s continued success. Sincerely, Ms. Mierzwik English Teacher	To the Parents of (Student's Name) (Address)

Jon is a boy who was in my class. He is good natured and boisterous. After the first two weeks of class, he had the highest grade point average of the class. I knew from speaking to his previous teacher that he generally struggled with school. I sent home a postcard sharing with his mother that he had the highest grade thus far in the year. Jon came to class after receiving the card excited, yet amazed. He told me he struggled in school, but since he had had such a great start, he wasn't going to slack off like usual. He was going to try to maintain his A.

It wasn't easy for Jon, but at the end of the first grading period, he still had an A. The postcard I sent home did several things. It recognized that Jon had completed every assignment to date, resulting in his high points earned. It recognized the effort Jon was making at the beginning of the school year with his good habits and his responsible behavior. It encouraged Jon to continue these behaviors. It worked. The previous year, Jon had barely passed with low C's. He passed my class with an A-. Three minutes of my time resulted in a school year of achievement and success for Jon.

The postcards also connect with parents. Time after time, students share with me that their parents have been so proud of them, that their parents rewarded them. Or, in the worst-case scenario, the child had been given a reprieve from the trouble she was in. When I meet with parents, they always mention the postcard they received, thanking me for taking the time to write it for them. I always respond in this situation with an explanation about how there is no need to thank me because their child deserved the recognition.

Spending a few minutes to send home a postcard builds your relationship with your student. It builds your relationship with the parent. It contributes positively to the relationship between your student and his or her parents.

Now that I've been using postcards for several years, I have fine-tuned how I use them. Instead of sending them home to the students who already get recognition in the class through their positive interactions with me and their classmates, I look for students who are introverted or struggling and make a point to recognize their effort early in the school year.

Joy is a quiet girl who doesn't interact much with her classmates. Her writing in my class was creative, but she was still struggling with mechanics. I wrote home a postcard praising her creative writing. Joy turned into the best author in the class and, by the end of the year, had poems published in anthologies for eighth graders and on several teen poetry Web sites. Last time I spoke to her, she was working on a novel.

Good news postcards acknowledge a child for their talent, effort, or achievement. They reinforce behaviors you find valuable within your classroom. They also get students on your side.

Cayla had an IEP from her resource teacher requiring me to make specific accommodations for her learning disability. I felt that her biggest disability was her attitude; she was angry. Many students after years of struggling and failing through school begin to act out as a means of self-preservation. The third week of school I sent a postcard home for Cayla, praising her effort and her high grade on a weekly quiz. Cayla's anger subsided. She still had an edge to her, but she trusted me as her teacher and continued to make an effort in my class all year. She no longer grew defensive every time I gave her directions. Three minutes of my time made an entire school year with a struggling student much more pleasant.

Sending Home Postcards

There are many reasons to send home a postcard. As with phone calls, the postcards need to be specific and sincere. I will choose to send a postcard home to a particular student and then spend the next several days watching for something positive that child does. As soon as I have something positive, I send home a postcard and wait for the magic to happen. Here are some reasons to send home a postcard:

- Behavior improvement
- Success on test or quiz
- Completed homework
- Highest grade in class
- Prepared to work
- Improved scores on tests, homework, classwork
- Great job on project
- Great oral presentation
- Helped another student
- Showed leadership qualities
- Showed empathy
- Set a good example for rest of class
- Made an extra effort
- Volunteered to help

There are many other reasons to send home a postcard. Just watch for good things, and you will find them.

Four short sentences that acknowledge a job well done will only take you a few minutes to write, but will help you to make a positive connection with the student and the student's parents.

Things to Remember

- Ask the secretary to print envelope labels for each of your students if possible
- The most current address will be found on the student's emergency release card
- Be sure that, if you address the postcard to the parents using their name, that you haven't assumed their last name is the same as the student's
- Most districts will allow you to send the postcards through district mail. Be sure to check with your site administrator
- You can create your own postcards by using the template at the back of this book and making copies on card stock

---

Reference

Barth, R. (1979). Home-based reinforcement of school behavior: A review and analysis. *Review of Educational Research, 49*, 436–458.

16

Inviting Parents to Visit

While I was in the middle of correcting the daily focus activity with the class, the phone rang in my classroom. I rushed to answer it, calming the class down and directing them to continue correcting their work using the answers on the overhead as I walked toward the beckoning ring. The school secretary was on the phone informing me that a parent was here to visit the class, unannounced, unscheduled. Was that okay with me?

If I refused, I could lose some credibility with the parent. What have I got to hide? If I agreed, I could lose some credibility with the parent. Does the parent understand this is not military school? Meanwhile, my students were growing restless.

The easiest way to avoid this dilemma is to invite parents to your class. Inviting parents before they show up unannounced means that you are able to set the tone, set the parameters, and prepare for the visit.

Having parents in your classroom allows parents to see firsthand how your class is structured, what type of relationship you have with your students, and how their children fit into the class. I once had a parent who was sure I was verbally abusing students in my class. Her daughter was going home and telling her some of the things I said in class. The mom went to the counselor and not only wanted her daughter out of the class, but also wanted me fired. The counselor invited her to visit my class. What she found was that I did say things like her daughter said I said such as when asked about the previous day's assignment and why it was not graded and I responded playfully, "No, I did not grade your papers last night. Excuse me for having a life," but in context these things were building relationships, not abusing students.

You may be reluctant to invite a parent to your class because you are afraid that the parent does not quite understand how a classroom works. Remember, the parent is a parent and understands how children work.

Sending Open Invitations

Times to invite a parent are varied. You can send out an open invitation for anytime, asking for notice if that makes you more comfortable.

Dear Parent,

Your ability to support your child in school depends on your understanding of the expectations and procedures of the classroom. One way to enhance your understanding of these things is to witness them firsthand. Visiting the classroom will allow you to see how our time together is organized, how classroom behavior is managed, and the basic structure of the class.

I realize that parents are very busy people and want you to know that if a classroom visit does not fit into your schedule, I am available to explain these things at another time.

If you are interested in visiting the classroom, I simply ask that you let me know at least a day before. With notice, I can alert the office of your visit so they are prepared for you. Your visit can be as long or as short as you would like.

Once again, I believe that working together to ensure the success of your child is so important. To help us work together, you are always welcome to visit.

Sincerely,

Ms. Mierzwik

If this seems intimidating to you, you should know a few things. First, very few parents generally will take you up on this offer, but it puts their mind at ease knowing that they are welcome in the class to observe at any time. Second, those parents who decide to visit probably were going to visit anyway and have that right, but by inviting them you have set the tone for the visit. Being proactive is always better than being defensive.

Inviting Parents to Volunteer in the Class

A way to get parents into your classroom in a nonthreatening manner is to invite them to volunteer. Not only does this allow parents to see firsthand how things are going in the class, but also the students enjoy the attention and help from other adults, theoretically it reduces your workload, and it creates an atmosphere of cooperation between home and school in your classroom.

Teachers at a local elementary school in my area send home a letter that looks like this:

We Need YOU!

Parents, you are the most influential person in your children's lives. You are the most important role model for your children. You can provide them with one-on-one interaction in their classroom by volunteering. Please check all the boxes where you can help. You'll be sent more information for each of the assignments you check.

❑ I'll help every other Monday with replacing bulletin boards.
❑ I can come every Friday from 10:00 to 11:00 to help students play games or write stories.
❑ I can come on Tuesdays from 9:00 to 10:00 for reading groups.
❑ I can come on Wednesday afternoons from 1:00 to 2:00 to help with science experiments.

Child's name _____

Parent signature _____

Phone # _____

The teachers who use this have set up specific times for parents to volunteer, which provides parents an opportunity to schedule the time into their week. They have also found that by specifying activities, the willingness of parents to volunteer has increased because parents can choose to visit the classroom during an activity that they find interesting.

One teacher shared with me that her classroom environment has improved since she began using parent volunteers in this manner. As a second-year teacher, she was intimidated at first, but once the parents began showing up, she found she felt so much at ease with them in the classroom that she and her students began looking forward to what they began calling "parent times."

Preparing for a Visit

When a parent does visit for observation, simply have a place for them to sit, perhaps at your desk since that seems to be the only place empty during class time. Let them know they are free to wander around the class. If the class is working on a project, you can even put the parent to work.

The students will love the interaction with an outsider and the parent will get a better sense of what your job entails.

Displaying for the parent your lesson plans, worksheets, or other materials being used that day helps the parent get a handle on what is happening in class. If you are keeping student portfolios, placing the parent's child's portfolio out is a good idea. The parent will have a chance to look through the types of assignments and assessments his or her child is completing in class. (Do not give the parent other student portfolios unless you hide that child's name.) If you keep student grades on a computer program, a print-out of the child's grade is also a good idea. Your goal in providing all of these documents is to help orient the parent to your class while you are busy teaching.

But the most important part of the visit is for the parent to observe how you interact with your students and how your students interact with one another. This can be very daunting for some teachers, especially if you are uncomfortable with your level of class control. Try to remember that the parent is there to support his or her child and you. The parent is not there to evaluate you. If you are doing the best you can, then you have nothing to hide. Parents deal with at least one child of that age every day. They have a clear understanding of what can be expected from children and their behavior.

I never change my lesson plans because a parent is visiting. If you find out at the last minute a parent is coming and you had silent reading planned but now want to change it because you are afraid the parent will think *that's not really teaching,* resist the urge. Changing your lesson plans will disrupt the students' schedule, making disruptive behavior more probable. Also, you will be distracted trying to make your changed lesson plan work, rather than naturally following your plans. You want parents to see you with your best foot forward. If the children are engaged in silent reading or watching a video, this gives you time to speak with the parent. Perhaps you could even send a student outside with the parent to read aloud or to explain how the video fits into the unit you are currently studying.

Inviting Parents for Class Presentations

Another great time to invite parents to visit is when students are giving presentations to the class. Inviting parents to watch oral presentations can be not only very gratifying for parents, but also very motivating for your students.

Once you have established which days the presentations are to be held, have students sign up for a given date and time. Then you can hand out preprinted invitations for students to fill out with their time and date to invite their parents to observe their presentation. The invitation could look like the one on the following page.

Dear Parents,

As you may be aware, our class is completing our unit on the ocean's ecosystem. As part of the unit, students will be giving oral presentations summarizing what they have learned as part of the unit.

We would like to invite you to join us. The presentations will be held on *dates* from *times*. Your child's presentations will be on *day* at *specific time*. Please feel free to come during any of the presentations.

Please RSVP by filling in the form below.

Thank you,

Ms. Mierzwik's class

I _____ will:

❑ not be able to attend
❑ be able to attend on _____ at _____ .

It will be important to alert the office that you may have visitors on these days so the secretaries are prepared to handle the extra visitor sign-ins or can make other arrangements. You may want to have your students make signs to post on campus to direct your parents to your classroom, or include a map of the school with your invitations. Be sure to let students know that not just parents but any adult who would like to visit is welcome.

Inviting Parents to Gain Support for a Difficult Child

Another time to invite parents to visit is when a child is having a difficult time conforming to classroom expectations. To gain parental support in this situation, it is important that the child perceive that you and his or her parents are working together to resolve the issue.

What happens when a child is having a difficult time conforming to classroom expectations? It is easy for the teacher to assume that the child is unable to follow classroom procedures because she is not required to behave in a similar manner at home. It is easy for the parent to assume that the child is having a difficult time at school because the teacher is unreasonable; after all, that is what the child has been saying for months. The truth lies somewhere between.

Children are masters at manipulating situations. I remember being in a parent-teacher conference—as the parent—and having the teacher attack me because I had told my son he wasn't learning anything at school; his teacher was wasting his time. I had to look the teacher straight in the eye, tell her my son had lied, and that he had manipulated her. He had her believing that I didn't support her, which resulted in him getting away with very poor behavior for over a month—until we were able to set things straight.

Had I been informed of my son's comment and resulting behaviors sooner, many bad habits would not have been formed in that classroom. Why didn't the teacher call me right away and invite me to witness how my son was behaving? I believed the teacher believed that my son's behavior was a result of my poor parenting skills and I would be of little help. My son was the one to suffer.

As teachers, it is not our job to assume that a child is misbehaving because of poor parenting. It is easy to do this, but as a parent of a not-so-easy child, I know firsthand that most parents are doing the best they can. I know I am. After going through this situation with my son, I realized that the assumption of poor parenting skills not only can be completely wrong, but does no one any good. As a teacher, you feel helpless, believing all the power resides with the parents. The parents feel accused and defensive and the child is left floundering, continuing to misbehave for the attention he so desperately needs.

The purpose of inviting a parent in this situation is so that the two of you can observe the situation, then brainstorm for solutions. It means that you must be willing to listen to a parent who is going to share with you what works for her when handling the child. This can be very empowering for you, the parent, and the child who needs consistency.

Usually these invitations need to be made in person or on the phone. The following conversation that could have taken place between my son's teacher and myself:

> Ms. Mierzwik, Wes is having a difficult time in class. He is out of his seat without permission. He is often off-task and he seems to need my constant attention to complete any work. I wonder what *I* could be doing differently to help Wes be more successful in class.

The parent will probably give you some suggestions about how to handle the child when he is acting difficult. She might even share with you some of the things the child is sharing with her about how the class is progressing. It is important to hear these things with an open mind. Do not grow defensive, but understand that this is the child's perception and perception is reality for a person. To continue with the previous example:

> I am surprised by how Wes is perceiving class. I want for Wes to be successful this year and I feel this misunderstanding is preventing that from happening. I wonder how you would feel about visiting the class one day to observe how Wes and I interact. Perhaps you can give me some guidance on what I can do differently to help Wes.

Some parents at this point will explain that you are the teacher and they trust your instincts. Others will be happy to come in, viewing it as an opportunity to help their child. Try to set up a time during the day when the child seems to be having the most difficulty, but be flexible with the parent's schedule. Also, try to arrange to debrief with the parent directly after the parental observation of the class.

Be prepared for several things to happen. First, the child will be on his best behavior. That doesn't matter. What matters is that the child sees you and the parent working together and is no longer able to divide and conquer as my son was trying to do. Second, the parent may have suggestions that seem unreasonable given the demands on our time with the curriculum and the other students. Listen attentively, take notes, and then see if there isn't some way you can incorporate some of the suggestions without compromising your classroom. Finally, the parent may shrug her shoulders, explaining she is at her wit's end also. At this point you will want to make a referral to the school's counseling program. In all of the aforementioned scenarios, the goal of the visit is accomplished; the student's needs are attended to by you and the parent.

Having parents visit your class can be intimidating, but it is also very empowering. As with any time you contact parents, you send the message that they are an important part of their child's education; that you value their input; and that, as a team, the two of you can ensure the success of their child. Also, you will be pleasantly surprised and rewarded not only with all the positive feedback you and your students receive from parents, but also from the amount of support parents will offer you once they understand that you respect and value their support.

Things to Remember

- Inviting parents to your classroom empowers you
- Parents have a right to visit
- General visits are helpful to clarify procedures
- Specific visits are great to showcase student achievement
- Visits to gain parental cooperation help students

17

Getting Attention
From the Media

Connecting with students and their parents is vital to the success of your students. Connecting with the public at large is vital to the success of education. As a professional educator, it sickens me every time teachers get bad press. It is true that often the bad press is accurate, but rarely does the media attention we get give the public a full picture.

This is not about making excuses for why we have low test scores, why there is so much violence in our schools, or why teacher turnover is so high. Other books deal with those issues. This is about sharing with the community the positive things that are happening in your classroom.

This chapter provides quick and easy ways to connect with your community. I do not suggest community nights that take hours of planning, organizing, and orchestrating. Further, I do not suggest that you join community committees that would require hours of your time to attend meetings. Instead, there are simple ways to extend what you are already doing in the class in order to share with your community.

If you are doing any other school activities, adults and students beyond your classroom already know about you. Your name comes up at the ball field, lunch, and family get-togethers. "How's school?" someone asks and the answer is "This year we have a teacher who really cares." You are gaining a reputation for being a teacher who is positive with students, who sets high standards and rewards students for reaching those high standards, and who listens to parents for input about how best to meet the needs of children.

I still remember a phone call I made to a parent whose son had disrupted final exams. Her answer was that everyone knew I hated boys, no wonder her child was acting out. I was astounded. I had no idea that I hated boys; being married to one and having one as a child made me absolutely fall in love with boys. I just didn't like her boy's behavior. But my reputation left me little room to discuss with her the problem her son was having in class.

Her mind was made up and I simply apologized that we had ended the year on such a sour note.

At the time I felt I had little control over what others were saying about me, about what type of reputation I was gaining. Not one parent had approached me about their concerns that I was biased toward girls so I had no way of combating the problem. And then it got thrown in my face. It would have been easy for me to decide the parent was incorrect in her accusation and move on with what I had always been doing. However, I knew I had done something to gain this reputation, however false I believed it to be.

I decided to take an active role in how others saw me as a teacher rather than letting parents draw conclusions from student stories and ballpark rumors. I began to use many of the activities in this book about connecting with parents so I wouldn't find out on the last day of the year that a parent was unhappy with me. But I also decided that when people spoke about me at the ball field, at church, or in the supermarket, I wanted people who didn't have firsthand experience with me to also have an idea of who I was.

Using Your Local Education Reporter

Most newspapers today have an education page. In my local newspaper it is located in the *Local* section, the second-to-last page. The section includes school menus; a class photo of a local class; "in brief," which includes fundraiser information or special events; and a larger article showcasing a special project by a class or school. This is an excellent resource for you as a teacher. If you have a student who has done something outstanding or your class or school has put on a program or created projects worth noticing, you will want to alert your local newspaper. Perhaps you just want your class to be chosen for the class photo. All you have to do is ask.

Most newspapers today have an education reporter. It is in your best interest to find out who this person is and to introduce yourself. Call the newspaper and ask for the education reporter, or simply read the paper and pay attention to the byline for all the articles about education. This reporter wants to know you. Part of a reporter's job is to get quotations regarding news items and to write about significant events within the local education system. Knowing you helps this person to do his or her job and also helps you to get some good press.

If you get the education reporter on the phone you will want to introduce yourself as a teacher. Let the reporter know which school you teach at, which positions you hold there (department head, school site member, etc.), and what grade or subject you teach. To build a relationship with the reporter, be sure to mention that you read her latest article and make a comment about how it was written well. Explain then that the purpose of the call is to find out which types of school events are noteworthy and to make yourself available to the reporter for articles.

The reporter will be thankful. She may direct you to another reporter on staff who handles local stories, but be sure she took down your name and information in case she ever needs you for comment on a story.

If the phone makes you nervous, you can do all this in a simple letter addressed to *Education Reporter.* The letter might look like this:

Date _____

Dear (Name if known),

I am a seventh- and eighth-grade English teacher at Parkview Middle School for Yucaipa-Calimesa Joint Unified School District. I recently read your article on the postponement of using the high school exit exam as a requirement for graduating titled, "Ruling on test rattles policy: Schools work to adjust graduation standards" in the July 14th paper. I couldn't help but wonder if the test requirement might be postponed again.

I'm writing to inquire about what types of school events you might be interested in covering for your paper. I know you have an *Education* page in the local section of the paper and am interested in having my class contribute to this page. I also would like to offer myself as a resource for you when you are writing about educational issues. I have been a teacher for 15 years, having taught in Yucaipa-Calimesa School District for the last 8 years. I have acted as department head, coordinator of GATE programs, Leadership team member, and as a mentor teacher over the years. As you can see, I have a varied background which gives me an informed perspective on issues. Please feel free to contact me at any time regarding school issues.

I look forward to hearing from you.

Diane Mierzwik

Phone number/e-mail address

Notice I've included my background, teaching experience, and experience with different facets of school programs. This allows the reporter to list you under resources with specific information about what you can knowledgeably comment on. However, the most important part of the letter is the request to share with the reporter the neat things that are going on in your class.

The reporter will likely give you some parameters to use when contacting the newspaper with events happening in your class. You will want to respect these parameters and not contact the reporter unless your activity fits into the scope of her reporting.

Using a Press Release

If your newspaper does not have an education reporter and you have not been able to make contact with a specific person on staff, yet something wonderful is happening in your class, you may want to write a press release. A press release is a convenient way to let newspapers know that something newsworthy is happening in your classroom.

Remember that the event in your class needs to be newsworthy. It can be as enormous as your class video project being aired on a public broadcast station or as small as one of your students being published in a poetry anthology. When newspapers are looking for education stories, they want to showcase students and teachers doing wonderful things. These stories are human interest stories. People read them to feel good about what's happening in the world.

Writing a press release is easy. The basic format is below and you will probably want to create a template of this format on your computer using your school district's letterhead.

School Letterhead

Immediate Release

Contact

Your name

Phone number where you can be reached (probably the school's)

Fax number if you have one

E-mail

Web site if you have one

Press Release

Headline (in bold)

200–500 words describing who, what, where, when, and how.

As you can see, the only work you have to do is to write the 200–500 words that describe what has happened that is newsworthy. I have often written much shorter press releases, but I make sure I include in the first paragraph all of the vitals; who, what, where, when, and how. I use the remainder of the release to fill in the story. Here is an example that resulted in a small article in the local newspaper:

Immediate Release

Contact

Your name: Diane Mierzwik

Phone number: (909) 790–3285

Fax number: (909) 790–3295

E-mail: msmezman@yahoo.com

Press Release

Yucaipa Junior High Students Become Published Authors

Jason Yodock, April Medsenes, and Terry Depret will all be published in the 2001 printing of *Young American Poets* published by Creative Communications, Inc.

Jason is an eighth-grade student at Yucaipa Junior High School who dreams of becoming a full-time author. "I'd like to write books for a living." His poem, "America Still Dreams" is one of many he has written.

April, also an eighth-grade student at YJHS, has been writing poetry since she was in fourth grade. "Whenever something is on my mind, writing a poem helps me to feel better," she says. April's poem, "Turning Around" was written after she was affected by the divorce of her parents.

Terry, a ninth grader at YJHS, was surprised his poem was selected for the publication. "I've never written poetry before," he says. His poem, "Tragedy" was written for his creative writing class. He says he may write more poems after this success.

From over 250,000 submissions, these three poets have had every writer's dream come true: publication.

I have written press releases for student publication, class publication, special visitors in my class, awards won by students beyond school contests, and special events such as oral presentations where students dress and act like an author. Some of my releases have been ignored. Some of been followed up by a reporter who wrote a small article. Some have been printed word for word. In any case, the press release took very little of my time and when it did garner some positive attention, it was worth the effort.

Using Other Newspaper Outlets

The *Letters to the Editor* section is a great place to get some publicity for your classroom. Taking the time to read this section and to respond to letters critical of the school system is well worth your effort. Responding to a negative article in the paper about schools is also a great way to get attention for what is going right with schools.

Writing a letter to the editor needs to be handled delicately. Try to avoid high emotions and stick to the facts. I have written letters responding to articles that claimed that smaller class sizes didn't improve student achievement and in response to readers who criticized student work published in the paper. In either case, I wrote a draft, let it sit a day or two, and then reread it for revising. I was careful that the language I chose was professional and to the point.

Be aware that often your letter will be cut to fit the space allotted for letters and your whole point may not come across—all the more reason to choose your words carefully so nothing can be taken out of context. Be prepared for responses to your letters, and be ready to back up your point of view without becoming unprofessional. After one letter I wrote, I received phone calls to my home all day. Needless to say, I was a bit surprised that these people had the time to find my phone number.

A less drastic way to use *Letters to the Editor* is to write a letter recognizing someone or something special that happened in your class. For instance, last Sunday a fourth-grade teacher from a local elementary school wrote a letter thanking the newspaper for the coverage they provided on her school's special event. Writing a letter to acknowledge parents who volunteered for a field trip, a donation provided to your class, or service above and beyond by school personnel or other agencies involved with your class makes the recognized people proud and assures the public that no good deed goes unnoticed in your classroom.

Once your letter is published, be sure to send a copy to each person or agency recognized in the letter. The letter should not replace a personal thank-you letter from you, but should be in addition to it.

If you are lucky, your newspaper also has a section that showcases children and their artwork or writing. In our newspaper it's a section called *Kidstuff* and is found at the back of the *Living* section. *Kidstuff* is run every Monday and is a great place for your students to showcase their talents. In my classroom, I have a bulletin board where I post each week's page and the address and requirements for submission. I also supply envelopes and mail submissions for my students. If I have students who are published on the page, these pieces are photocopied and posted on the bulletin board with the child's name highlighted.

Usually the child's school name is listed with his or her grade. Not only does the child feel great about being published in the paper and parents are proud of their child's accomplishment, but also it generates positive attention for your school. It's a wonderful way to publicize what great students you have in your class.

Gaining Outside Recognition for Students

Beyond your local newspaper, there are many opportunities for your students to participate in contests. Usually contests for children center on drawing something or writing something short. I watch all the time for contests that would be appropriate for my students.

I've had students win money in essay contests, get published in books, get published on the Internet, and receive certificates of recognition. There is such a sense of pride for a student who is recognized for his or her work beyond the school setting. The affirmation of a job well done by someone other than parents or teachers has a great effect on a student's perceptions of his or her abilities. And in the process your class and school gets some well-deserved recognition for providing support for the child's talents.

Managing these types of activities can be daunting. I provide copies of the entry forms to all my students when I find an activity and then post the due date for my class on the board. The due date for my class is usually a week or so before the actual due date. That gives me time to be sure the work is in the proper format. Then I mail the entries for the students. I rarely make these assignments requirements, but occasionally I will allow the assignment to count for another class assignment. For instance, if you submit an entry to the contest, you can skip Thursday night's homework.

I have had classes in which it is difficult to keep up with the student entries and classes in which no one takes any interest in submitting entries. I leave it up to the class. When students do take part in the contests, it doesn't matter to me if they win. What matters is that the children have had an opportunity to take part in something beyond the school setting using their talents and have represented our class and our school with pride. It is one more opportunity to gain some recognition for the hard work you and your students do each day in class.

Making the effort to extend many of the things you are already doing to connect with the public is worth the few minutes it takes to gain recognition for yourself and your students. If by spending a few minutes we can make a positive impression on someone's perception of the school system, we have made a connection that is invaluable.

Things to Remember

- Be proactive in building your reputation
- Use your local newspaper to gain attention
- Always present yourself to others professionally
- Create opportunities for students to get recognition for special work
- Offer opportunities for students to explore their talents with contests

Resource

Sample Forms and Letters

Sample Congratulations Certificate

Congratulations!

_____

has received this certificate of merit for a job well done in

_____

presented on this _____ day of _____ in the year _____

by

_____

Sample Introduction Letter 1

Date _____

Dear Parents or Guardians,

Welcome to the new school year and my classroom. I am looking forward to a successful year with your child and want to assure you that I am prepared for a wonderful experience.

I hold a Bachelor of Arts in English from the University of California, Riverside where I also earned my teaching credential. I also have done post graduate work in Education Administration and English Composition. I have participated in many professional trainings, most notably the Inland Empire Writing Project and as a Language Arts Consultant for California Language Arts Project. I have been teaching for over 15 years.

My goal this year is to help your child build on the skills and knowledge attained last year and to extend those successes to future success. I will work diligently to be sure that all students in my classroom master the grade-level standards. Student work will often have a reference to which standard the work is aimed at. If you are interested in viewing the standards for this grade level, feel free to contact me or visit www.ca.edu.standards.

My classroom policies are very simple. Students have homework every night. If a child explains that he or she has already finished the homework, the child should be reading for pleasure for at least 20 minutes. My classroom expectation for students is that each student does his or her best work. I am available for extra help before and after school to ensure that every child is successful. If your child is going to be absent for an extended amount of time, please contact me so we can prepare the child for his or her return to the classroom.

It is important to me that we work together to ensure your child's success. Please feel free to contact me before or after school or by e-mail. I will do my best to respond within 24 hours.

Sincerely,

Ms. Mierzwik

E-mail/phone number

I have read and understand the policies outlined in the above letter.

_____
Student Signature

_____
Parent Signature

Sample Parent Letter 2

Parents,

Welcome to a new year. My name is Ms. Huffs and I am very excited about the new school year and teaching your child. I know that this year will be a very successful and challenging year for all!

I have taught in Ontario/Montclair for 13 years and have been employed by Beaumont for the last 6 years. I love teaching and I know that all children will learn, achieve, and feel successful in my classroom.

Please read the following rules and policies with your child.

Classroom Rules

1. Respect yourself and others.
2. Raise your hand to speak.
3. Do not interrupt or disturb others who are working.
4. Follow directions.

Discipline/Consequences

I have a color chart in the classroom which is used for discipline. All students begin each day on green and colors are changed according to behavior.

Green = Excellent

Blue = Warning

Orange = Loss of recess

Red = Lunch detention

Excessive Problems = Principal referral and/or telephone call home

Students' behavior grades are based on how many times they change a color on the behavior chart. All students are given 10 points each week and 1 point is deducted for each time a color is changed.

Homework

Students will be given a school planner and be expected to record their homework assignments each day. This is so parents may check assignments if necessary. Students will then be responsible for taking their work home, completing their work and returning it every day. Homework credit will be given for homework that is completed and returned on time. Credit will not be given for late work unless there is an absence or emergency.

(Continued)

(Continued)

Book Report/Reading Log

Each student will also be responsible for completing a book report and a reading log each week. These will be due on Fridays.

Progress Reports

Following the first few weeks of school, after students have had a chance to familiarize themselves to the assignments and the requirements in my classroom, I will be sending home weekly progress reports. These will show how your child is doing both academically and behaviorally in my class. These letters will go home every Monday or Tuesday showing the previous week's work. These will need to be signed and returned the following day.

I look forward to an exciting year. Please feel free to contact me at anytime.

Ms. Huffs

Please sign, detach, and return the bottom portion

- -

Student Name _____

Behavior Plan Acknowledgment:

I have received and reviewed the Classroom Behavior Plan with my child.

Parent/Guardian Signature _____

Date _____

Comments/Questions:

Sample Parent Survey K–2

Your Child as a Learner (K–2)

Name _____ Date _____

Grade _____ Class _____

Please indicate your observation of your child's learning behaviors in the following areas. Please provide explanations or examples where appropriate.

My Child	*Yes/No*	*Comments/ Examples*
1. Enjoys "playing" with language		
• Listens to		
• Participates in		
• Stories		
• Poems and rhymes		
2. Communicates with others		
• About own activities		
• About information discovered		
• Explaining ideas clearly		
• In community talk		
3. Expresses ideas:		
• In an understandable way		
• In an appropriate way		
4. Is aware of some print conventions		
• Capital letters		
• End punctuation (periods, etc.)		
• Text and picture carry a story		
5. Is interested in school		
6. Learns from watching others		

(Continued)

(Continued)

7. Voluntarily engages in:		
• Reading		
• Writing		
• Problem solving		
8. Appears confident about learning		
9. Cooperates with others		
10. Can count orally to . . .		
11. Is able to manipulate objects in number groups		

If there is any additional information that you think might help me to better know your child as a student, please feel free to write on the back of this page or on another paper.

Thank you for your help. I look forward to working with you this year.

Sample Parent Survey 3–5

Your Child as a Learner (3–5)

Name _____ Date _____

Grade _____ Class _____

Please indicate your observation of your child's learning behaviors in the following areas. Please provide explanations or examples where appropriate.

My Child	Yes/No	Comments/ Examples
1. Chooses to read		
• For pleasure		
• Favorite books repeatedly		
• For information		
• Challenging text		
2. Communicates with others		
• About own activities		
• About information discovered		
• Explaining ideas clearly		
• In community talk		
3. Expresses ideas:		
• Adjusting speaking patterns to audience		
• In an understandable way		
4. Displays control over mechanics		
• Punctuation		
• Grammatical constructions		
• Spelling of high-frequency words		
5. Monitors understanding of spoken language by asking questions		

(Continued)

(Continued)

6. Is able to summarize text for retelling		
7. Is productive and involved during		
• Homework time		
• Personal time		
• Problem solving		
8. Appears confident about learning		
9. Plans, organizes, and carries through on tasks		
10. Differentiates between relevant and nonrelevant information		
11. Understands that not all problems have simple solutions		

If there is any additional information that you think might help me to better know your child as a student, please feel free to write on the back of this page or on another paper.

Thank you for your help. I look forward to working with you this year.

Sample Parent Survey 6–8

Your Child as a Learner (6–8)

Name _____ Date _____

Grade _____ Class _____

Please indicate your observation of your child's learning behaviors in the following areas. Please provide explanations or examples where appropriate.

My Child	Yes/No	Comments/Examples
1. Makes responsible choices about:		
• Listening (music, radio, conversation)		
• Reading (books, magazines, newspapers)		
• Viewing (TV, movies, posters, catalogs)		
• Playing (video games, PC games)		
2. Voluntarily shares his/her:		
• Drawing		
• Writing		
• Talking		
• Creative projects		
3. Expresses ideas:		
• In an understandable way		
• In an appropriate way		
4. Expresses opinions about:		
• Reading		
• TV programs, movies		
• Ideas presented at school		

(Continued)

(Continued)

5. Independently seeks information		
6. Persists in tasks		
7. Voluntarily engages in:		
• Reading		
• Writing		
• Problem solving		
8. Appears confident about learning		
9. Learns from errors		
10. Likes to read about . . .		
11. Likes to write about . . .		

If there is any additional information that you think might help me to better know your child as a student, please feel free to write on the back of this page or on another paper.

Thank you for your help. I look forward to working with you this year.

Sample Student Survey

Yourself as a Learner

Name _____ Date _____

Grade _____ Class _____

Please indicate your behaviors in the following areas. Please provide explanations or examples where appropriate.

I	*Yes/No*	*Comments/ Examples*
1. Make responsible choices about:		
• Listening (music, radio, conversation)		
• Reading (books, magazines, newspapers)		
• Viewing (TV, movies, posters, catalogs)		
• Playing (video games, PC games)		
2. Voluntarily share my:		
• Drawing		
• Writing		
• Talking		
• Creative projects		
3. Express ideas:		
• In an understandable way		
• In an appropriate way		
4. Express opinions about:		
• Reading		
• TV programs, movies		
• Ideas presented at school		
5. Independently seek information		

(Continued)

(Continued)

6. Persist in tasks		
7. Voluntarily engage in:		
• Reading		
• Writing		
• Problem solving		
8. Am confident about learning		
9. Learn from errors		
10. Like to read about . . .		
11. Like to write about . . .		

If there is any additional information that you think might help me to better know you as a student, please feel free to write on the back of this page or on another paper.

Thank you for your help. I look forward to working with you this year.

Sample Request for Parent Letter About Child

Date _____

Dear Parent or Guardian,

I'm very enthusiastic about working with your child this year. I have an exciting school year planned and look forward to watching each of my students grow and learn during their time with me.

It would help me to know about your child from your perspective. You are in the unique position of observing your child outside the school situation and can give me many insights into their habits and behaviors, likes and dislikes, and interests. With this information, I will be able to manage, monitor, and adjust the curriculum to be sure it is meeting the needs of your child. Success breeds success and I want your child to be successful in my class.

Please spend a few minutes writing a letter explaining to me your child's homework habits, interests in school and out of school, how your child has done in school in the past and any techniques used by previous teachers that were successful with your child.

If you have any questions, please feel free to contact me.

Sincerely,

Diane Mierzwik

Phone number

Sample Classroom Procedure Letter

Dear Parent and Student,

Welcome to Ms. Mierzwik's class. I hope that, like me, you had a wonderful break and are looking forward to a very successful year. To make this year a success, it is important that every student be held to high expectations. I want my expectations to be very clear.

I expect every student to be prepared for class each day with the proper supplies, including writing utensils, paper, and the proper books. It helps if students have a notebook for class and a backpack to carry all belongings.

I will be assigning homework Monday through Thursday. If a student feels that he or she has no homework, the student should spend time reading for the assigned book report or future projects. Occasionally, a student may have to work on a project over the weekend if he or she has not been able to budget weekday time accordingly.

If a student is absent, the child has the number of days absent upon returning to complete all make-up work. I would strongly urge that for an extended absence I be contacted for missed work so the student does not feel overwhelmed.

Late work is accepted for partial credit if turned in within a week of the due date. Work turned in later than a week will be accepted only on a case-by-case basis.

Adherence to classroom behavioral expectations is expected from all students. When a child has a difficult day, time-out in another classroom may be used along with a parent notification. If the problem persists other consequences will follow.

Grades are based on the child's ability to meet the grade-level standards as evidenced by class work, homework, assessments, and teacher evaluations of performance in class. I will do my best to keep you informed of your child's progress.

I look forward to working with each student and am anticipating another successful year. If you have any questions, please feel free to contact me.

Sincerely,

Ms. Mierzwik

Sample Request for Parent
Suggestions for Classroom Procedures

Dear Parent,

As we reach the end of the third week of class, I wanted to check in with you about your child's progress in my class. As you know, I feel it is very important that we work together to ensure the success of your child, which requires that we communicate openly and frequently about how things are progressing. I want to remind you of a few things about class and then would like your feedback regarding how these things are affecting your child.

Please remember that I hold every child to the highest expectations in class, but am willing to make accommodations to help to ensure that your child can do his or her best work. Homework is an important part of the curriculum. It helps your child practice skills, extend information and create new knowledge. Finally, your child's perception of class is important to his or her motivation. I want your child to feel capable and valuable in class.

If you could take the time to fill out the bottom part of this letter, providing feedback when necessary, it would help me to be sure that your child is progressing successfully with the curriculum, expectations, and procedures of class. You may want to discuss this survey with your child. If there is a concern, please share that with me honestly. I will do my best to address your concern. Finally, if you would rather speak to me in person, feel free to call so that we can set up an appointment to meet.

Thank you for your continued support,

Ms. Mierzwik

- -

Child's Name _____

1. My child feels comfortable with the pace of the class: yes / no
2. My child is able to complete the homework with   yes / no
   little or no help:
3. The time it takes my child to complete homework is   yes / no
   reasonable:
4. My child feels confident that he/she can be   yes / no
   successful in class:

If you answered no to any questions, please explain or provide a phone number and time to reach you.

Sample Request for Parent Suggestions for Unit/Quarter

Dear Parent,

We have just completed first quarter. We had a successful quarter with completion of our *House on Mango Street* project, our first book report and our end of the quarter assessments.

To help me plan for second quarter, I would like your perception of how things went. If you have suggestions for ways I could have made the quarter more successful for your child, I would like you to share these with me. I strive to make my class a positive experience for every child and your help in this endeavor is invaluable.

Please take a moment to complete the bottom survey and return it with your child. As with any time I ask for your input, if there are concerns, feel free to explain them here, to leave a phone number and time I can reach you, or to call the school to set up a time we can meet to discuss your concerns.

I know that with your continued support, we can continue our success into the second quarter.

Thanks,

Ms. Mierzwik

- -

Child's Name _____

1. The homework load was reasonable: yes / no

2. The homework extended or affirmed learning: yes / no

3. Directions for units and projects were clear: yes /no

4. Large assignments were organized so that students   yes / no
   were able to complete smaller units of the
   assignment before the final project was due:

5. My child feels capable in class: yes / no

6. My child feels able to ask for extra help in class: yes / no

7. My child had a successful quarter: yes / no

Please feel free to comment on any of the above or to contact me with any concerns. Thanks.

Sample Thank-You Letters

Back to School Night Thank-You

Dear _____ ,

I want to thank you for attending Back-to-School Night last Thursday. I know how busy parents are and making time in your schedule to attend shows me that you are very involved in your child's education. I wish I had had more time to speak to you individually. If you have any questions or concerns, please feel free to contact me.

Once again, thanks for your attendance.

Sincerely,

Supportive Parent Thank-You

Dear Mr. Jensen,

Joey explained to me in class today that you took him to the book store so he could buy a book to read for his book report. Thank you so much for helping Joey fulfill the requirements for my class. Your support will help him to be successful in class. The book he chose sounds interesting. I can't wait to read his report.

Sincerely,

Joey's Teacher

Follow-Up to Parent Contact Thank-You

Dear Mr. and Mrs. Fedro,

Thank you for taking time out of your busy day to discuss Samantha's education with me at the conference on Tuesday. I appreciate how we were able to set up a plan to help Samantha be more successful in my class. I will continue to work to help Samantha stay on task during classroom time. I think that having you check her weekly progress report will help Samantha. If there is anything else you need from me, or if a modification of the plan is needed, please feel free to contact me.

Sincerely,

Samantha's Teacher

Child Serving Consequence Thank-You

Dear Mr. Rouse,

Thank you for supporting me in my efforts to keep Albert on task during class time. When Albert is focused in class, he is very successful and it is important to me that Albert is successful in class. He served his detention last Thursday. We spent the time working on some missing assignments and discussing ways for Albert to stay focused during class time. I appreciate your support in my efforts to make sure Albert has a productive year.

Sincerely,

Albert's Teacher

Sample Letter Regarding E-mail Communication

Date _____

Dear Parents,

To ensure your child's success in my class this year, I feel very strongly about being able to communicate with you about important due dates and expectations. I also want to be available to you if you have any questions or concerns regarding your child, class projects and activities, or class expectations.

One way for us to communicate easily is through the use of e-mail. I realize that not every parent has e-mail and if you do not have e-mail, rest assured that I am always available through a phone call. For those parents who do have e-mail, if you would like to use this vehicle as a means to keep in contact with me, it is a very easy process to set up.

My e-mail address is _____ . If you would like me to use e-mail as a way to keep you informed, please e-mail me a message indicating this and I will be able to add your e-mail address to my address book. I will use e-mail to inform you of upcoming due dates and activities in class, as well as to inform you of any specific information I feel you need regarding your child.

I believe the success of your child in my class depends on a good working relationship between the school and family. Being able to communicate with you is very important to me. I hope that the use of e-mail will provide one more way for us to work together toward a productive year.

I look forward to e-mail messages from those of you who are able to take advantage of this technology, but once again want to assure parents who do not have this technology that I will be available in other ways for you.

Thank you,

Diane Mierzwik

Letter Confirming E-mail Message

Dear _____

Thank you for contacting me via e-mail. I look forward to using this technology to keep you updated on your child's progress as well as important due dates and activities occurring in class.

If you ever have a question, please feel free to contact me using this account. I will be diligent about responding to e-mail and try to get back to you within 24 hours.

I look forward to a successful year with your child.

Sincerely,

E-mail Message Regarding Needing Parent Contact

Dear _____

Today in class, _____ seemed distracted. To ensure his success, I would like to speak to you about the situation. I tried to contact you by phone (date and time) but (answering machine, voice message, busy signal, no answer).

I can be reached at school before and after school or during my conference period from _____ to _____ , or feel free to contact me at home. My number is _____ and the best time to reach me is between _____ . If these times are not convenient for you, please let me know when would be a good time to contact you.

In the past, _____ has done a good job in class and I want to be sure that he continues to be successful.

I look forward to speaking with you about this situation.

Thank you,

E-mail Message About Student Poor Performance

Dear _____

_____ has (name a specific thing the child does well in class) received a 100% on homework thus far in the year. I was very concerned yesterday when she did not have her homework completed for the week. This is unlike her. I want to offer my help to solve any problem that prevented her from completing the homework.

Please let me know what I can do to help solve this situation. _____ is welcome to turn the assignment in late for partial credit unless there were some extenuating circumstances.

Sincerely,

E-mail Message Regarding Student Poor Behavior

Dear _____

Thank you for responding to my e-mail. The concern I had about _____ was his behavior in class. Unfortunately, _____ chose to talk out of turn many times today. I repeatedly redirected his behavior, but I'm unsure if he understood how distracting he was for the other students and me.

_____ has been quiet and attentive in the past and I know that when he is motivated, he can act appropriately in class. If there is something I can do to help motivate him to make better choices during class time, I would be happy to do so. As it stands, if his behavior continues, he will be assigned a consequence.

I know that working together, we can help _____ be successful in school.

Let me know what I can do to help.

Sincerely,

Sample Good News Postcards

Dear Parents of _____

I just wanted you to know that _____ received the highest grade in her class for this grading period. I am very proud of _____ and enjoy having her in class.

Sincerely,

Date _____

Dear Parents of _____ ,

I just wanted you to know how proud I am of _____ .
This week _____ turned in all of her homework on time. It is so wonderful to see _____ acting responsibly about her work. I am looking forward to _____'s continued success.

Sincerely,

Ms. Mierzwik

English Teacher

To the Parents of
(Student's Name)
(Address)

Sample Letter to Education Reporter

Date _____

Dear (Name if known),

I am a seventh- and eighth-grade English teacher at Parkview Middle School for Yucaipa Calimesa Joint Unified School District. I recently read your article on the postponement of using the high school exit exam as a requirement for graduating titled, "Ruling on test rattles policy: Schools work to adjust graduation standards" in the July 14th paper. I couldn't help but wonder if the test requirement might be postponed again.

I'm writing to inquire about what types of school events you might be interested in covering for your paper. I know you have an *Education* page in the local section of the paper and am interested in having my class contribute to this page. I also would like to offer myself as a resource for you when you are writing about educational issues. I have been a teacher for 15 years, having taught in Yucaipa-Calimesa School District for the last 8 years. I have acted as department head, coordinator of GATE programs, Leadership team member and as a mentor teacher over the years. As you can see, I have a varied background which gives me an informed perspective on issues. Please feel free to contact me at any time regarding school issues.

I look forward to hearing from you.

Diane Mierzwik

Phone number/e-mail address

Sample Press Release

School Letterhead

Immediate Release

Contact

Your name

Phone number where you can be reached (probably the school's)

Fax number if you have one

E-mail

Web site if you have one

Press Release

Headline (in bold)

200–500 words describing who, what, where, when, and how.

Sample Phone Log

Month _____ Teacher _____

Grade _____ Room _____

Date	Name of Student	Type of Contact	Who Was Reached	Comments

Index

**CORWIN
PRESS**

The Corwin Press logo—a raven striding across an open book—represents the union of courage and learning. Corwin Press is committed to improving education for all learners by publishing books and other professional development resources for those serving the field of K–12 education. By providing practical, hands-on materials, Corwin Press continues to carry out the promise of its motto: **"Helping Educators Do Their Work Better."**